PHP 7 Quick Scripting Reference

Second Edition

Mikael Olsson

Apress®

PHP 7 Quick Scripting Reference

Mikael Olsson
Hammarland,
Finland

ISBN-13 (pbk): 978-1-4842-1921-8   ISBN-13 (electronic): 978-1-4842-1922-5
DOI 10.1007/978-1-4842-1922-5

Library of Congress Control Number: 2016941199

Managing Director: Welmoed Spahr
Lead Editor: Steve Anglin
Technical Reviewer: Jamie Rumbelow
Editorial Board: Steve Anglin, Pramila Balan, Louise Corrigan, Jonathan Gennick,
    Robert Hutchinson, Celestin Suresh John, Michelle Lowman, James Markham,
    Susan McDermott, Matthew Moodie, Jeffrey Pepper, Douglas Pundick,
    Ben Renow-Clarke, Gwenan Spearing
Coordinating Editor: Mark Powers
Copy Editor: Kim Burton-Weisman
Compositor: SPi Global
Indexer: SPi Global
Artist: SPi Global

Distributed to the book trade worldwide by Springer Science+Business Media New York, 233 Spring Street, 6th Floor, New York, NY 10013. Phone 1-800-SPRINGER, fax (201) 348-4505, e-mail orders-ny@springer-sbm.com, or visit www.springeronline.com. Apress Media, LLC is a California LLC and the sole member (owner) is Springer Science + Business Media Finance Inc (SSBM Finance Inc). SSBM Finance Inc is a Delaware corporation.

For information on translations, please e-mail rights@apress.com, or visit www.apress.com.

Apress and friends of ED books may be purchased in bulk for academic, corporate, or promotional use. eBook versions and licenses are also available for most titles. For more information, reference our Special Bulk Sales–eBook Licensing web page at www.apress.com/bulk-sales.

Any source code or other supplementary materials referenced by the author in this text is available to readers at www.apress.com/9781484219218. For detailed information about how to locate your book's source code, go to www.apress.com/source-code/. Readers can also access source code at SpringerLink in the Supplementary Material section for each chapter.

Printed on acid-free paper

Contents at a Glance

iii

Contents

About the Author

Mikael Olsson is a professional web entrepreneur, programmer, and author. He works for an R&D company in Finland, where he specializes in software development.

In his spare time, Mikael writes books and creates web sites on his various fields of interest. The books that he writes are focused on efficiently teaching the subject by explaining only what is relevant and practical, without any unnecessary repetition or theory.

About the Technical Reviewer

Jamie Rumbelow is a freelance web developer and an aspiring academic. He's the author of three books on CodeIgniter and is a keen public speaker. He has worked on dozens of web applications during his eight years freelancing. Jamie lives in London, England.

Introduction

PHP is a server-side programming language used for creating dynamic web sites and interactive web applications. The acronym PHP originally stood for Personal Home Page, but as its functionality grew, this was changed to PHP: Hypertext Preprocessor. This recursive acronym comes from the fact that it takes PHP code as input and produces HTML as output. This means that users do not need to install any software to view PHP-generated web pages. All that is required is that the web server has PHP installed to interpret the script.

In contrast with HTML sites, PHP sites are dynamically generated. Instead of the site being made up of a large number of static HTML files, a PHP site may consist of only a handful of template files. The template files describe only the structure of the site using PHP code, while the web content is pulled from a database and the style formatting is from Cascading Style Sheets (CSS). This allows for site-wide changes from a single location, providing a flexible web site that is easy to design, maintain, and update.

When creating web sites with PHP, a content management system (CMS) is generally used. A CMS provides a fully integrated platform for web site development consisting of a back end and a front end. The front end is what visitors see when they arrive at the site, whereas the back end is where the site is configured, updated, and managed by an administrator. The back end also allows a web developer to change template files and modify plugins to more extensively customize the functionality and structure of the site. Examples of free PHP-based CMS solutions include WordPress, Joomla, ModX, and Drupal, with WordPress being the most popular and accounting for more than half of the CMS market.

The first version of PHP was created by Rasmus Lerdorf and released in 1995. Since then, PHP has evolved greatly from a simple scripting language to a fully featured web programming language. The official implementation is now released by The PHP Group, with PHP 7 being the most recent version as of this writing. The language may be used free of charge and is open source, allowing developers to extend it for their own use or to contribute to its development.

PHP is by far the most popular server-side programming language in use today. It holds a growing 80% market share when compared with other server-side technologies, such as ASP.NET, Java, Ruby, and Perl. One of the reasons for the widespread adoption of PHP is its platform independence. It can be installed on all major web servers and operating systems, and used with any major database system. Another strong feature of PHP is its simple-to-use syntax based on C and Perl, which is easy for a newcomer to learn; however, PHP also offers many advanced features for the professional programmer.

CHAPTER 1

Using PHP

To start developing in PHP, create a plain text file with a .php file extension and open it in the editor of your choice—for example Notepad, jEdit, Dreamweaver, NetBeans, or PHPEclipse. This PHP file can include any HTML, as well as PHP scripting code. Begin by first entering the following minimal markup for an HTML 5 web document.

```
<!doctype html>
<html>
 <head>
  <meta charset="UTF-8">
  <title>PHP Test</title>
 </head>
 <body></body>
</html>
```

Embedding PHP

PHP code can be embedded anywhere in a web document in several different ways. The standard notation is to delimit the code by <?php and ?>. This is called a *PHP code block*, or just a *PHP block*.

```
<?php ... ?>
```

Within a PHP block, the engine is said to be in *PHP mode*; outside of the block, the engine is in *HTML mode*. In PHP mode, everything is parsed (executed) by the PHP engine; whereas in HTML mode, everything is sent to the generated web page without any execution.

Electronic supplementary material The online version of this chapter (doi:10.1007/978-1-4842-1922-5_1) contains supplementary material, which is available to authorized users.

The second notation for switching to PHP mode is a short version of the first where the php part is left out. Although this notation is shorter, the longer one is preferable if the PHP code needs to be portable. This is because support for the short delimiter can be disabled in the php.ini configuration file.[1]

```
<? ... ?>
```

A third (now obsolete) alternative was to embed the PHP code within an HTML script element with the language attribute set to php. This alternative delimiter was seldom used; support for it was removed in PHP 7.

```
<script language="php">...</script>
```

Another obsolete notation that you may encounter in legacy code is when the script is embedded between ASP tags. This notation is disabled by default, but it can be enabled from the PHP configuration file. Use of this notation has long been discouraged. The ability to enable it was finally removed in PHP 7.

```
<% ... %>
```

The last closing tag in a script file may be omitted to make the file end while it is still in PHP mode.

```
<?php ... ?>
<?php ...
```

Outputting Text

Printing text in PHP is done by either typing **echo** or **print** followed by the output. Each statement must end with a semicolon (;) in order to separate it from other statements. The semicolon for the last statement in a PHP block is optional, but it is a good practice to include it.

```
<?php
  echo "Hello World";
  print "Hello World";
?>
```

Output can also be generated using the <?= open delimiter. As of PHP 5.4, this syntax is valid even if the short PHP delimiter is disabled.

```
<?= "Hello World" ?>
```

---

[1]http://www.php.net/manual/en/configuration.file.php

Keep in mind that text displayed on a web page should always be located within the HTML body element.

```
<body>
  <?php echo "Hello World"; ?>
</body>
```

Installing a Web Server

To view PHP code in a browser, the code first has to be parsed on a web server with the PHP module installed. An easy way to set up a PHP environment is to download and install a distribution of the popular Apache web server called XAMPP,[2] which comes preinstalled with PHP, Perl, and MySQL. It allows you to experiment with PHP on your own computer.

After installing the web server, point your browser to `http://localhost` to make sure that the server is online. It should display the `index.php` file, which by default is located under `C:\xampp\htdocs\index.php` on a Windows machine. `htdocs` is the folder that the Apache web server looks to for files to serve on your domain.

Hello World

Continuing from before, the simple Hello World PHP web document should look like this:

```
<!doctype html>
<html>
 <head>
  <meta charset="UTF-8">
  <title>PHP Test</title>
 </head>
 <body>
  <?php echo "Hello World"; ?>
 </body>
</html>
```

To view this PHP file parsed into HTML, save it to the web server's `htdocs` folder (the server's root directory) with a name such as `mypage.php`. Then point your browser to its path, which is `http://localhost/mypage.php` for a local web server.

When a request is made for the PHP web page, the script is parsed on the server and sent to the browser as only HTML. If the source code for the web site is viewed, it will not show any of the server-side code that generated the page—only the HTML output.

---

[2]`http://www.apachefriends.org/en/xampp.html`

3

Compile and Parse

PHP is an interpreted language, not a compiled language. Every time a visitor arrives at a PHP web site, the PHP engine compiles the code and parses it into HTML, which is then sent to the visitor. The main advantage of this is that the code can be changed easily without having to recompile and redeploy the web site. The main disadvantage is that compiling the code at run-time requires more server resources.

For a small web site, a lack of server resources is seldom an issue. The time it takes to compile the PHP script is also miniscule compared to other factors, such as the time required to execute database queries. However, for a large web application with lots of traffic, the server load from compiling PHP files is likely to be significant. For such a site, the script compilation overhead can be removed by precompiling the PHP code. This can be done with eAccelerator,[3] for example, which caches PHP scripts in their compiled state.

A web site that only serves static content (the same to all visitors) has another possibility, which is to cache the fully generated HTML pages. This provides all the maintenance benefits of having a dynamic site, with the speed of a static site. One such caching tool is the W3 Total Cache[4] plugin for the WordPress CMS.

Comments

Comments are used to insert notes into the code. They have no effect on the parsing of the script. PHP has the two standard C++ notations for single-line (//) and multiline (/* */) comments. The Perl comment notation (#) may also be used to make single-line comments.

```php
<?php
  // single-line comment
  #  single-line comment
  /* multi-line
     comment */
?>
```

As in HTML, whitespace characters—such as spaces, tabs, and comments—are ignored by the PHP engine. This allows you a lot of freedom in how to format your code.

---

[3]http://www.eaccelerator.net
[4]http://wordpress.org/extend/plugins/w3-total-cache

CHAPTER 2

Variables

Variables are used for storing data, such as numbers or strings, so that they can be used multiple times in a script.

Defining Variables

A variable starts with a dollar sign ($) followed by an *identifier*, which is the name of the variable. A common naming convention for variables is to have each word initially capitalized, except for the first one.

```
$myVar;
```

A value can be assigned to a variable by using the equals sign, or assignment operator (=). The variable then becomes *defined* or *initialized*.

```
$myVar = 10;
```

Once a variable has been defined, it can be used by referencing the variable's name. For example, the value of the variable can be printed to the web page by using echo followed by the variable's name.

```
echo $myVar; // "10"
```

Keep in mind that variable names are case sensitive. Names in PHP can include underscore characters and numbers, but they cannot start with a number. They also cannot contain spaces or special characters, and they must not be a reserved keyword.

Data Types

PHP is a loosely typed language. This means that the type of data that a variable can store is not specified. Instead, a variable's data type changes automatically to hold the value that it is assigned.

```
$myVar = 1;   // int type
$myVar = 1.5; // float type
```

© Mikael Olsson 2016
M. Olsson, *PHP 7 Quick Scripting Reference*, DOI 10.1007/978-1-4842-1922-5_2

Furthermore, the value of a variable is evaluated differently, depending on the context in which it is used.

```
// Float type evaluated as string type
echo $myVar; // "1.5"
```

Because of these implicit type conversions, knowing the underlying type of a variable is not always necessary. Nevertheless, it is important to have an understanding of the data types that PHP works with in the background. These nine types are listed in Table 2-1.

Table 2-1. *PHP Data Types*

Data Type	Category	Description
int	Scalar	Integer
float	Scalar	Floating-point number
bool	Scalar	Boolean value
string	Scalar	Series of characters
array	Composite	Collection of values
object	Composite	User-defined data type
resource	Special	External resource
callable	Special	Function or method
null	Special	No value

Integer Type

An integer is a whole number. They can be specified in decimal (base 10), hexadecimal (base 16), octal (base 8) or binary (base 2) notation. Hexadecimal numbers are preceded with a 0x, octal with a 0, and binary numbers with a 0b.

```
$myInt = 1234; // decimal number
$myInt = 0b10; // binary number (2 decimal)
$myInt = 0123; // octal number (83 decimal)
$myInt = 0x1A; // hexadecimal number (26 decimal)
```

Integers in PHP are always signed and can therefore store both positive and negative values. The size of an integer depends on the system word size, so on a 32-bit system, the largest storable value is 2^{32-1}. If PHP encounters a larger value, it is interpreted as a float instead.

Floating-Point Type

The float or floating-point type can store real numbers. These can be assigned using either decimal or exponential notation.

```
$myFloat = 1.234;
$myFloat = 3e2; // 3*10^2 = 300
```

The precision of a float is platform dependent. Commonly, the 64-bit IEEE format is used, which can hold approximately 14 decimal digits and a maximum decimal value of 1.8×10^{308}.

Bool Type

The bool type can store a Boolean value, which is a value that can only be either true or false. These values are specified with the true and false keywords.

```
$myBool = true;
```

Null Type

The case-insensitive constant null is used to represent a variable with no value. Such a variable is considered to be of the special null data type.

```
$myNull = null; // variable is set to null
```

Just as with other values, the null value evaluates differently, depending on the context in which the variable is used. If evaluated as a bool, it becomes false; as a number, it becomes zero (0); and as a string, it becomes an empty string ("").

```
$myInt = $myNull + 0;       // numeric context (0)
$myBool = $myNull == true;  // bool context     (false)
echo $myNull;               // string context   ("")
```

Default Values

In PHP, it is possible to use variables that have not been assigned a value. Such undefined variables are then automatically created with the null value.

```
echo $myUndefined; // variable is set to null
```

Although this behavior is allowed, it is a good coding practice to define variables before they are used, even if the variables are just set to null. As a reminder for this, PHP issues an error notice when undefined variables are used. Depending on the PHP error reporting settings, this message may or may not be displayed.

```
Notice: Undefined variable: myUndefined in C:\xampp\htdocs\mypage.php on
line 10
```

CHAPTER 3

Operators

An operator is a symbol that makes the script perform a specific mathematical or logical manipulation. The operators in PHP can be grouped into five types: arithmetic, assignment, comparison, logical, and bitwise operators.

Arithmetic Operators

The arithmetic operators include the four basic arithmetic operations, as well as the modulus operator (%), which is used to obtain the division remainder.

```php
$x = 4 + 2; // 6 // addition
$x = 4 - 2; // 2 // subtraction
$x = 4 * 2; // 8 // multiplication
$x = 4 / 2; // 2 // division
$x = 4 % 2; // 0 // modulus (division remainder)
```

An exponentiation operator (**) was introduced in PHP 5.6. It raises the left-side operand to the power of the right-side operand.

```php
$x = 4 ** 2; // 16 // exponentiation
```

Assignment Operators

The second group is the assignment operators. Most importantly, the assignment operator (=) itself, which assigns a value to a variable.

```php
$x = 1; // assignment
```

© Mikael Olsson 2016

M. Olsson, *PHP 7 Quick Scripting Reference*, DOI 10.1007/978-1-4842-1922-5_3

Combined Assignment Operators

A common use of the assignment and arithmetic operators is to operate on a variable and then to save the result back into that same variable. These operations can be shortened with the combined assignment operators.

```
$x += 5; // $x = $x+5;
$x -= 5; // $x = $x-5;
$x *= 5; // $x = $x*5;
$x /= 5; // $x = $x/5;
$x %= 5; // $x = $x%5;
```

The exponentiation operator added in PHP 5.6 also received a shorthand assignment operator.

```
$x **= 5; // $x = $x**5;
```

Increment and Decrement Operators

Another common operation is to increment or decrement a variable by one. This can be simplified with the increment (++) and decrement (--) operators.

```
$x++; // $x += 1;
$x--; // $x -= 1;
```

Both of these operators can be used either before or after a variable.

```
$x++; // post-increment
$x--; // post-decrement
++$x; // pre-increment
--$x; // pre-decrement
```

The result on the variable is the same whichever is used. The difference is that the post-operator returns the original value before it changes the variable, whereas the pre-operator changes the variable first and then returns the value.

```
$x = 5; $y = $x++; // $x=6, $y=5
$x = 5; $y = ++$x; // $x=6, $y=6
```

Comparison Operators

The comparison operators compare two values and return either true or false. They are mainly used to specify conditions, which are expressions that evaluate to either true or false.

```
$x = (2 == 3);  // false // equal to
$x = (2 != 3);  // true  // not equal to
$x = (2 <> 3);  // true  // not equal to (alternative)
$x = (2 === 3); // false // identical
$x = (2 !== 3); // true  // not identical
$x = (2 > 3);   // false // greater than
$x = (2 < 3);   // true  // less than
$x = (2 >= 3);  // false // greater than or equal to
$x = (2 <= 3);  // true  // less than or equal to
```

The strict equality operators, === and !==, are used for comparing both type and value. These are necessary because the regular "equal to" (==) and "not equal to" (!=) operators automatically perform a type conversion before they compare the operands. It is considered good practice to use strict comparison when the type conversion feature of the "equal to" operation is not needed.

```
$x = (1 ==  "1"); // true  (same value)
$x = (1 === "1"); // false (different types)
```

PHP 7 added a new comparison operator called the *spaceship operator* (<=>). It compares two values and returns 0 if both values are equal; 1 if the value on the left side is greater; and –1 if the value on the right side is greater.

```
$x = 1 <=> 1; // 0 (1 == 1)
$x = 1 <=> 2; //-1 (1 < 2)
$x = 3 <=> 2; // 1 (3 > 2)
```

Logical Operators

The logical operators are often used together with the comparison operators. Logical and (&&) evaluates to true if both the left and right side are true, and logical or (||) evaluates to true if either the left or right side is true. For inverting a Boolean result, there is the logical not (!) operator. Note that for both "logical and" and the "logical or", the right side of the operator is not evaluated if the result is already determined by the left side.

```
$x = (true && false); // false // logical and
$x = (true || false); // true  // logical or
$x = !(true);         // false // logical not
```

Bitwise Operators

The bitwise operators can manipulate binary digits of numbers. For example, the xor operator (^) turn on the bits that are set on one side of the operator, but not on both sides.

```
$x = 5 & 4;  // 101 & 100 = 100 (4) // and
$x = 5 | 4;  // 101 | 100 = 101 (5) // or
$x = 5 ^ 4;  // 101 ^ 100 = 001 (1) // xor (exclusive or)
$x = 4 << 1; // 100 << 1  =1000 (8) // left shift
$x = 4 >> 1; // 100 >> 1  =  10 (2) // right shift
$x = ~4;     // ~00000100 = 11111011 (-5) // invert
```

These bitwise operators have shorthand assignment operators, just like the arithmetic operators.

```
$x=5; $x &= 4;  // 101 & 100 = 100 (4) // and
$x=5; $x |= 4;  // 101 | 100 = 101 (5) // or
$x=5; $x ^= 4;  // 101 ^ 100 = 001 (1) // xor
$x=5; $x <<= 1; // 101 << 1  =1010 (10)// left shift
$x=5; $x >>= 1; // 101 >> 1  =  10 (2) // right shift
```

Note that decimal numbers used together with binary operators are automatically converted to binary. The binary notation may also be used to specify binary numbers for the operation.

```
$x = 0b101 & 0b100; // 0b100 (4)
```

Operator Precedence

When an expression contains multiple operators, the precedence of those operators decides the order in which they are evaluated. The order of precedence can be seen in Table 3-1.

Table 3-1. *Order of Operator Precedence*

Pre	Operator	Pre	Operator
1	**	10	&
2	++ --	11	^
3	~ - (unary)	12	|
4	!	13	&&
5	* / %	14	||
6	+ - (binary)	15	= op=
7	<< >>	16	and
8	< <= > >= <>	17	xor
9	== != === !== <=>	18	or

To give an example, multiplication has greater precedence than addition, and therefore it is evaluated first in the following line of code.

```
$x = 4 + 3 * 2; // 10
```

Parentheses can be used to force precedence. An expression placed within parentheses is evaluated before other expressions in that statement.

```
$x = (4 + 3) * 2; // 14
```

Additional Logical Operators

In the precedence table, make special note of the last three operators: and, or, and xor. The and and or operators work in the same way as the logical && and || operators. The only difference is their lower level of precedence.

```
// Same as: $a = (true && false);
$x = true && false; // $x is false

// Same as: ($a = true) and false;
$x = true and false; // $x is true
```

The xor operator is a Boolean version of the bitwise ^ operator. It evaluates to true if only one of the operands are true.

```
$x = (true xor true); // false
```

CHAPTER 4

String

A string is a series of characters that can be stored in a variable. In PHP, strings are often delimited by single quotes.

```php
$a = 'Hello';
```

String Concatenation

PHP has two string operators. The dot symbol is known as the *concatenation operator* (.). It combines two strings into one. It also has an accompanying assignment operator (.=), which appends the right-hand string to the left-hand string variable.

```php
$b = $a . ' World'; // Hello World
$a .= ' World';     // Hello World
```

Delimiting Strings

PHP strings can be delimited in four different ways. There are two common notations: double quote (" ") and single quote (' '). The difference between them is that variables are not parsed in single-quoted strings, whereas they are parsed in double-quoted strings.

```php
$c = 'World';
echo "Hello $c"; // "Hello World"
echo 'Hello $c'; // "Hello $c"
```

Single-quoted strings tend to be preferred unless parsing is desired, which highlights that no parsing takes place. However, double-quoted strings are considered easier to read, which makes the choice more a matter of preference. The important thing is to be consistent.

In addition to single-quoted and double-quoted strings, there are two more notations: *heredoc* and *nowdoc*. These notations are mainly used to include larger blocks of text.

© Mikael Olsson 2016
M. Olsson, *PHP 7 Quick Scripting Reference*, DOI 10.1007/978-1-4842-1922-5_4

Heredoc Strings

The heredoc syntax consists of the <<< operator followed by an identifier and a new line. The string is then included followed by a new line containing the identifier to close the string. Variables are parsed inside of a heredoc string, just as with double-quoted strings.

```
$s = <<<LABEL
Heredoc (with parsing)
LABEL;
```

Nowdoc Strings

The syntax for the nowdoc string is the same as for the heredoc string, except that the initial identifier is enclosed in single quotes. Variables are not parsed inside a nowdoc string.

```
$s = <<<'LABEL'
Nowdoc (without parsing)
LABEL;
```

Escape Characters

Escape characters are used to write special characters, such as backslashes and double quotes. These characters are always preceded by a backslash (\). Table 4-1 lists the escape characters available in PHP.

Table 4-1. *The Escape Characters Available in PHP*

Character	Meaning	Character	Meaning
\n	newline	\f	form feed
\t	horizontal tab	\$	dollar sign
\v	vertical tab	\'	single quote
\e	escape	\"	double quote
\r	carriage return	\\	backslash
\u{}	Unicode character		

For example, line breaks are represented with the escape character (\n) within strings.

```
$s = "Hello\nWorld";
```

Note that this character is different from the `<br>` HTML tag, which creates line breaks on web pages.

```
echo "Hello<br>World";
```

When using the single quote or nowdoc delimiter, the only escape characters that work are the backslash (\\) and single-quote (\') characters. Escaping the backslash is only necessary before a single quote or at the end of the string.

```
$s = 'It\'s'; // "It's"
```

PHP 7 introduced the Unicode escape character, which provides the ability to embed UTF-8 encoded characters into strings. Such a character is specified as a hexadecimal number inside curly brackets. The number can be up to six digits long, with leading zeros being optional.

```
echo "\u{00C2A9}"; // © (copyright sign)
echo "\u{C2A9}";   // ©
```

Character Reference

Characters within strings can be referenced by specifying the index of the desired character in square brackets after the string variable, starting with zero. This can be used both for accessing and modifying single characters.

```
$s = 'Hello';
$s[0] = 'J';
echo $s; // "Jello"
```

The `strlen` function retrieves the length of the string argument. This can be used to change the last character of a string, for example.

```
$s[strlen($s)-1] = 'y';
echo $s; // "Jelly"
```

String Compare

The way to compare two strings is simply by using one of the equality operators. This does not compare the memory addresses, as in some other languages.

```
$a = 'test';
$b = 'test';
$c = ($a === $b); // true
```

CHAPTER 5

Arrays

An array is used to store a collection of values in a single variable. Arrays in PHP consist of key-value pairs. The key can either be an integer (numeric array), a string (associative array), or a combination of both (mixed array). The value can be any data type.

Numeric Arrays

Numeric arrays store each element in the array with a numeric index. An array is created using the `array` constructor. This constructor takes a list of values, which are assigned to elements of the array.

```
$a = array(1,2,3);
```

As of PHP 5.4, a shorter syntax is available, where the array constructor is replaced with square brackets.

```
$a = [1,2,3];
```

Once the array is created, its elements can be referenced by placing the index of the desired element in square brackets. Note that the index begins with zero.

```
$a[0] = 1;
$a[1] = 2;
$a[2] = 3;
```

The number of elements in the array is handled automatically. Adding a new element to the array is as easy as assigning a value to it.

```
$a[3] = 4;
```

The index can also be left out to add the value to the end of the array. This syntax also constructs a new array if the variable does not already contain one.

```
$a[] = 5; // $a[4]
```

© Mikael Olsson 2016
M. Olsson, *PHP 7 Quick Scripting Reference*, DOI 10.1007/978-1-4842-1922-5_5

To retrieve the value of an element in the array, the index of that element is specified inside the square brackets.

```
echo "$a[0] $a[1] $a[2] $a[3]"; // "1 2 3 4"
```

Associative Arrays

In associative arrays, the key is a string instead of a numeric index, which gives the element a name instead of a number. When creating the array the double arrow operator (=>) is used to tell which key refers to what value.

```
$b = array('one' => 'a', 'two' => 'b', 'three' => 'c');
```

Elements in associative arrays are referenced using the element names. They cannot be referenced with a numeric index.

```
$b['one']   = 'a';
$b['two']   = 'b';
$b['three'] = 'c';

echo $b['one'] . $b['two'] . $b['three']; // "abc"
```

The double arrow operator can also be used with numeric arrays to decide in which element a value is placed.

```
$c = array(0 => 0, 1 => 1, 2 => 2);
```

Not all keys need to be specified. If a key is left unspecified, the value is assigned to the element following the largest previously used integer key.

```
$e = array(5 => 5, 6);
```

Mixed Arrays

PHP makes no distinction between associative and numerical arrays, and so elements of each can be combined in the same array.

```
$d = array(0 => 1, 'foo' => 'bar');
```

Just be sure to access the elements with the same keys.

```
echo $d[0] . $d['foo']; // "1bar"
```

Multi-Dimensional Arrays

A multi-dimensional array is an array that contains other arrays. For example, a two-dimensional array can be constructed in the following way.

```
$a = array(array('00', '01'), array('10', '11'));
```

Once created, the elements can be modified using two sets of square brackets.

```
$a[0][0] = '00';
$a[0][1] = '01';
$a[1][0] = '10';
$a[1][1] = '11';
```

They are also accessed in the same way.

```
echo $a[0][0] . $a[0][1] . $a[1][0] . $a[1][1];
```

The key can be given a string name to make it into a multi-dimensional associative array, also called a *hash table*.

```
$b = array('one' => array('00', '01'));
echo $b['one'][0] . $b['one'][1]; // "0001"
```

Multi-dimensional arrays can have more than two dimensions by adding additional sets of square brackets.

```
$c[][][][] = "0000"; // four dimensions
```

CHAPTER 6

Conditionals

Conditional statements are used to execute different code blocks based on different conditions.

If Statement

The if statement only executes if the condition inside the parentheses is evaluated to true. The condition can include any of the comparison and logical operators. In PHP, the condition does not have to be a Boolean expression.

```php
if ($x == 1) {
  echo "x is 1";
}
```

To test for other conditions, the if statement can be extended with any number of elseif clauses. Each additional condition is only tested if all previous conditions are false.

```php
elseif ($x == 2) {
  echo "x is 2";
}
```

For handling all other cases, there can be one else clause at the end, which executes if all previous conditions are false.

```php
else {
  echo "x is something else";
}
```

The curly brackets can be left out if only a single statement needs to be executed conditionally. However, it is considered good practice to always include them since they improve code readability.

```
if ($x == 1)
  echo "x is 1";
elseif ($x == 2)
  echo "x is 2";
else
  echo "x is something else";
```

Switch Statement

The switch statement checks for equality between an integer, float, or string and a series of case labels. It then passes execution to the matching case. The statement can contain any number of case clauses and may end with a default label for handling all other cases.

```
switch ($x)
{
  case 1: echo "x is 1"; break;
  case 2: echo "x is 2"; break;
  default: echo "x is something else";
}
```

Note that the statements after each case label are not surrounded by curly brackets. Instead, the statements end with the break keyword to break out of the switch. Without the break, the execution falls through to the next case. This is useful if several cases need to be evaluated in the same way.

Alternative Syntax

PHP has an alternative syntax for the conditional statements. In this syntax, the if statement's opening bracket is replaced with a colon, the closing bracket is removed, and the last closing bracket is replaced with the endif keyword.

```
if ($x == 1):    echo "x is 1";
elseif ($x == 2): echo "x is 2";
else:            echo "x is something else";
endif;
```

Similarly, the switch statement also has an alternative syntax, which instead uses the endswitch keyword to terminate the statement.

```
switch ($x):
  case 1:  echo "x is 1"; break;
  case 2:  echo "x is 2"; break;
  default: echo "x is something else";
endswitch;
```

The alternative syntax is often preferable for longer conditional statements since it then becomes easier to see where those statements end.

Mixed Modes

It is possible to switch back to HTML mode in the middle of a code block. This provides another way of writing conditional statements that output text to the web page.

```php
<?php if ($x == 1) { ?>
  This will show if $x is 1.
<?php } else { ?>
  Otherwise this will show.
<?php } ?>
```

The alternative syntax may also be used in this way to make the code clearer.

```php
<?php if ($x == 1): ?>
  This will show if $x is 1.
<?php else: ?>
  Otherwise this will show.
<?php endif; ?>
```

When outputting HTML and text, particularly larger blocks, this coding style is generally preferred because it makes it easier to distinguish between PHP code and the HTML content that appears on the web page.

Ternary Operator

In addition to the if and switch statements, there is the ternary operator (?:). This operator can replace a single if/else clause. The operator takes three expressions. If the first one is evaluated to true, then the second expression is returned, and if it is false, the third one is returned.

```php
// Ternary operator expression
$y = ($x == 1) ? 1 : 2;
```

In PHP, this operator be used as an expression and as a statement.

```php
// Ternary operator statement
($x == 1) ? $y = 1 : $y = 2;
```

The programming term *expression* refers to code that evaluates to a value, whereas a *statement* is a code segment that ends with a semicolon or a closing curly bracket.

CHAPTER 7

Loops

There are four looping structures in PHP. These are used to execute a specific code block multiple times. Just as with the conditional if statement, the curly brackets for the loops can be left out if there is only one statement in the code block.

While Loop

The while loop runs through the code block only if its condition is true. It continues looping for as long as the condition remains true. Note that the condition is only checked at the beginning of each iteration (loop).

```php
$i = 0;
while ($i < 10) { echo $i++; } // 0-9
```

Do-while Loop

The do-while loop works in the same way as the while loop, except that it checks the condition after the code block. Therefore, it always runs through the code block at least once. Bear in mind that this loop ends with a semicolon.

```php
$i = 0;
do { echo $i++; } while ($i < 10); // 0-9
```

For Loop

The for loop is used to go through a code block a specific number of times. It uses three parameters. The first parameter initializes a counter and is always executed once, before the loop. The second parameter holds the condition for the loop and is checked before each iteration. The third parameter contains the increment of the counter and is executed at the end of each iteration.

```php
for ($i = 0; $i < 10; $i++) { echo $i; } // 0-9
```

The for loop has several variations since either one of the parameters can be left out. For example, if the first and third parameters are left out, it behaves in the same way as the while loop.

```
for (;$i < 10;) { echo $i++; }
```

The first and third parameters can also be split into several statements using the comma operator (,).

```
for ($i = 0, $x = 9; $i < 10; $i++, $x--) {
  echo $x; // 9-0
}
```

The sizeof function retrieves the number of elements in an array. Together with the for loop, it can be used to iterate through a numeric array.

```
$a = array(1,2,3);

for($i = 0; $i < sizeof($a); $i++) {
  echo $a[$i]; // "123"
}
```

If there is no need to keep track of iterations, the foreach loop provides a cleaner syntax. This loop is also necessary for traversing associative arrays.

Foreach Loop

The foreach loop provides an easy way to iterate through arrays. At each iteration, the next element in the array is assigned to the specified variable (the iterator) and the loop continues to execute until it has gone through the entire array.

```
$a = array(1,2,3);

foreach ($a as $v) {
  echo $v; // "123"
}
```

There is an extension of the foreach loop to also obtain the key's name or index by adding a key variable followed by the double arrow operator (=>) before the iterator.

```
$a = array('one' => 1, 'two' => 2, 'three' => 3);

foreach ($a as $k => $v) {
  echo "$k => $v <br>";
}
```

Alternative Syntax

As with conditional statements, the brackets in the loops can be rewritten into the alternative syntax with a colon and one of the endwhile, endfor, or endforeach keywords.

```
while ($i < 10): echo $i++; endwhile;

for ($i = 0; $i < 10; $i++): echo $i; endfor;

foreach ($a as $v): echo $v; endforeach;
```

The main benefit of this is improved readability, especially for longer loops.

Break

There are two special keywords that can be used inside loops—break and continue. The break keyword ends the execution of a loop structure.

```
for (;;) { break; } // end for
```

It can be given a numeric argument that specifies how many nested looping structures to break out of.

```
$i = 0;
while ($i++ < 10)
{
  for (;;) { break 2; } // end for and while
}
```

Continue

The continue keyword can be used within any looping statement to skip the rest of the current loop and continue at the beginning of the next iteration.

```
while ($i++ < 10) { continue; } // start next iteration
```

This keyword can accept an argument for how many enclosing loops it should skip to the end of.

```
$i = 0;
while ($i++ < 10)
{
  for (;;) { continue 2; } // start next while iteration
}
```

In contrast to many other languages, the continue statement also applies to switches, where it behaves the same as break. Therefore, to skip an iteration from inside a switch, continue 2 needs to be used.

```
$i = 0;
while ($i++ < 10)
{
  switch ($i)
  {
    case 1: continue 2; // start next while iteration
  }
}
```

Goto

A third jump statement introduced in PHP 5.3 is goto, which performs a jump to a specified label. A label is a name followed by a colon (:).

```
goto myLabel; // jump to label
myLabel:      // label declaration
```

The target label must be within the same script file and scope. Therefore, goto cannot be used to jump into looping structures, only out of them.

```
loop:
while (!$finished)
{
  // ...
  if ($try_again) goto loop; // restart loop
}
```

In general, the goto statement is often best avoided since it tends to make the flow of execution difficult to follow.

CHAPTER 8

Functions

Functions are reusable code blocks that only execute when called. They allow the code to be divided into smaller parts that are easier to understand and reuse.

Defining Functions

To create a function, the `function` keyword is used, followed by a name, a set of parentheses, and a code block. The naming convention[1] for functions is the same as for variables—to use a descriptive name with each word initially capitalized, except for the first one.

```php
function myFunc()
{
  echo 'Hello World';
}
```

A function code block can contain any valid PHP code, including other function definitions.

Calling Functions

Once defined, a function can be called (invoked) from anywhere on the page by typing its name followed by a set of parenthesis. Function names are case insensitive, but it is good practice to use the same casing that they have in their definition.

```php
myFunc(); // "Hello World"
```

A function can be called even if the function definition appears further down in the script file.

```php
foo(); // ok
function foo() {}
```

---

[1]http://www.php-fig.org/psr/psr-2/

© Mikael Olsson 2016
M. Olsson, *PHP 7 Quick Scripting Reference*, DOI 10.1007/978-1-4842-1922-5_8

An exception to this is where the function is only defined when a certain condition is met. That conditional code must then be executed prior to calling the function.

```
bar(); // error
if (true) { function bar() {} }
bar(); // ok
```

Function Parameters

The parentheses that follow the function name are used to pass arguments to the function. To do this, the corresponding parameters must first be specified in the function definition in the form of a comma-separated list of variables. The parameters can then be used in the function.

```
function myFunc($x, $y)
{
  echo $x . $y;
}
```

With the parameters specified, the function can be called with the same number of arguments.

```
myFunc('Hello', ' World'); // "Hello World"
```

To be precise, *parameters* appear in function definitions, whereas *arguments* appear in function calls. However, the two terms are sometimes used interchangeably.

Default Parameters

It is possible to specify default values for parameters by assigning them a value inside the parameter list. Then, if that argument is unspecified when the function is called, the default value is used instead. For this to work as expected, it is important that the parameters with default values are declared to the right of those without default values.

```
function myFunc($x, $y = ' Earth')
{
  echo $x . $y;
}

myFunc('Hello'); // "Hello Earth"
```

Variable Parameter Lists

A function cannot be called with fewer arguments than is specified in its declaration, but it may be called with more arguments. This allows for the passing of a variable number of arguments, which can then be accessed using a couple of built-in functions. For getting one argument at a time, there is the func_get_arg function. This function takes a single argument, which is the parameter to be returned, starting with zero.

```
function myArgs()
{
  $x = func_get_arg(0);
  $y = func_get_arg(1);
  $z = func_get_arg(2);
  echo $x . $y . $z;
}

myArgs('Fee', 'Fi', 'Fo'); // "FeeFiFo"
```

There are two more functions related to the argument list. The func_num_args function gets the number of arguments passed and func_get_args returns an array containing all of those arguments. Together they can be used to allow a function to handle a variable number of arguments.

```
function myArgs2()
{
  $num  = func_num_args();
  $args = func_get_args();
  for ($i = 0; $i < $num; $i++)
    echo $args[$i];
}

myArgs2('Fee', 'Fi', 'Fo'); // "FeeFiFo"
```

The use of variable parameter lists were simplified in PHP 5.6. As of this version, parameter lists may include a variadic parameter, indicated by an ellipsis (...) token, which accepts a variable number of arguments. The variadic parameter behaves as an array and must always be the last parameter in the list.

```
function myArgs3(...$args)
{
  foreach($args as $v) {
    echo $v;
  }
}

myArgs3(1, 2, 3); // "123"
```

As a complementary feature, the ellipsis token can also be used to unpack a collection of values into an argument list.

```
$a = [1, 2, 3];
myArgs3(...$a); // "123"
```

Return Statement

return is a jump statement that causes the function to end its execution and return to the location where it was called.

```
function myFunc()
{
  return;    // exit function
  echo 'Hi'; // never executes
}
```

It can optionally be given a value to return, in which case it makes the function call evaluate to that value.

```
function myFunc()
{
  // Exit function and return value
  return 'Hello';
}

echo myFunc(); // "Hello"
```

A function without a return value automatically returns null.

```
function myNull() {}

if (myNull() === null)
  echo 'true'; // "true"
```

Scope and Lifetime

Normally, a PHP variable's scope starts where it is declared and lasts until the end of the page. However, a local function scope is introduced within functions. By default, any variable used inside a function is limited to this local scope. Once the scope of the function ends, the local variable is destroyed.

```
$x = 'Hello'; // global variable

function myFunc()
{
  $y = ' World'; // local variable
}
```

In PHP, trying to access a global variable from a function does not work and instead creates a new local variable. In order to make a global variable accessible, the scope of that variable must be extended to the function by declaring it with the global keyword.

```
$x = 'Hello'; // global $x

function myFunc()
{
  global $x;      // use global $x
  $x .= ' World'; // change global $x
}

myFunc();
echo $x; // "Hello World"
```

An alternative way to access variables from the global scope is by using the predefined $GLOBALS array. The variable is referenced by its name, specified as a string without the dollar sign.

```
function myFunc()
{
  $GLOBALS['x'] .= ' World'; // change global $x
}
```

In contrast to many other languages, control structures—such as loop and conditional statements—do not have their own variable scope. Therefore, a variable defined in such a code block is not destroyed when the code block ends.

```
if(true)
{
  $x = 10; // global $x
}

echo $x; // "10"
```

In addition to global and local variables, PHP also has property variables; these are looked at in the next chapter.

Anonymous Functions

PHP 5.3 introduced *anonymous functions*, which allow functions to be passed as arguments and assigned to variables. An anonymous function is defined like a regular function, except that it has no specified name. The function can be assigned to a variable using the normal assignment syntax, including the semicolon. That variable can then be called as a function.

```
$say = function($name)
{
  echo "Hello " . $name;
};

$say("World"); // "Hello World"
```

Anonymous functions are mainly used as *callback functions*. This is a function passed as an argument to another function, which is expected to call it as part of its execution.

```
function myCaller($myCallback)
{
  echo $myCallback();
}

// "Hello"
myCaller( function() { echo "Hello"; } );
```

In this way, functionality can be injected into an existing function, increasing its versatility. For instance, the built-in array_map function applies its callback to each element of its given array.

```
$a = [1, 2, 3];

$squared = array_map(function($val)
{
  return $val * $val;
}, $a);

foreach ($squared as $v)
  echo $v; // "149"
```

A benefit of using anonymous functions is that they allow for a concise way to define functions that are only used once in the location where they are used. This also prevents such throwaway functions from cluttering up the global scope.

Closures

A closure is an anonymous function that can capture variables local to the scope it was created in. In PHP, all anonymous functions are closures. They can specify variables to be captured with a use clause in the function header.

```php
$x = 1;
$y = 2;

$myClosure = function($z) use ($x, $y)
{
  return $x + $y + $z;
};

echo $myClosure(3); // "6"
```

Generators

A *generator* is a function used to generate a series of values. Each value is returned with a yield statement. Unlike return, the yield statement saves the state of the function, allowing it to continue from where it left off when it is called again.

```php
function getNum()
{
  for ($i = 0; $i < 5; $i++) {
    yield $i;
  }
}
```

The generator function behaves as an iterator; therefore, it can be used with a foreach loop. The loop continues until the generator has no more values to yield.

```php
foreach(getNum() as $v)
  echo $v; // "01234"
```

Generators were introduced in PHP 5.5. Their use was expanded in PHP 7 with the yield from statement, which allows a generator to yield values from another generator, iterator, or array.

```php
function countToFive()
{
  yield 1;
  yield from [2, 3, 4];
  yield 5;
}

foreach (countToFive() as $v)
  echo $v; // "12345"
```

Since generators only yield values one at a time on demand, they do not require the whole sequence to be computed all at once and stored in memory. This can have significant performance benefits when it comes to generating large amounts of data.

Built-in Functions

PHP comes with a large number of built-in functions that are always available, such as string and array handling functions. Other functions depend on what extensions PHP is compiled with; for example, the MySQLi extension for communicating with MySQL databases. For a complete reference of the built-in PHP functions, see the PHP Function Reference.[2]

---

[2]http://www.php.net/manual/en/funcref.php

CHAPTER 9

Class

A *class* is a template used to create objects. To define one, the class keyword is used, followed by a name and a code block. The naming convention for classes is mixed case, meaning that each word should be initially capitalized.

```
class MyRectangle {}
```

The class body can contain properties and methods. *Properties* are variables that hold the state of the object, whereas *methods* are functions that define what the object can do. Properties are also known as *fields* or *attributes* in other languages. In PHP, they need to have an explicit access level specified. In the following, the public access level is used, which gives unrestricted access to the property.

```
class MyRectangle
{
  public $x, $y;
  function newArea($a, $b) { return $a * $b; }
}
```

To access members from inside the class, the $this pseudo variable is used along with the single arrow operator (->). The $this variable is a reference to the current instance of the class and can only be used within an object context. Without it, $x and $y would just be seen as local variables.

```
class MyRectangle
{
  public $x, $y;

  function newArea($a, $b)
  {
    return $a * $b;
  }
```

```
  function getArea()
  {
    return $this->newArea($this->x, $this->y);
  }
}
```

Instantiating an Object

To use a class's members from outside the enclosing class, an object of the class must first be created. This is done using the new keyword, which creates a new object or instance.

```
$r = new MyRectangle(); // object instantiated
```

The object contains its own set of properties, which can hold values that are different from those of other instances of the class. As with functions, objects of a class may be created even if the class definition appears further down in the script file.

```
$r = new MyDummy(); // ok
class MyDummy {};
```

Accessing Object Members

To access members that belong to an object, the single arrow operator (->) is needed. It can be used to call methods or to assign values to properties.

```
$r->x = 5;
$r->y = 10;
$r->getArea(); // 50
```

Another way to initialize properties is to use initial property values.

Initial Property Values

If a property needs to have an initial value, a clean way is to assign the property at the same time that it is declared. This initial value is then set when the object is created. Assignments of this kind must be a constant expression. It cannot, for example, be a variable or a mathematical expression.

```
class MyRectangle
{
  public $x = 5, $y = 10;
}
```

Constructor

A class can have a constructor, which is a special method used to initialize (construct) the object. This method provides a way to initialize properties, which is not limited to constant expressions. In PHP, the constructor starts with two underscores followed by the word construct. Methods like these are known as *magic methods*.

```php
class MyRectangle
{
  public $x, $y;

  function __construct()
  {
    $this->x = 5;
    $this->y = 10;
    echo "Constructed";
  }
}
```

When a new instance of this class is created, the constructor is called, which in this example sets the properties to the specified values. Note that any initial property values are set before the constructor is run.

```php
$r = new MyRectangle(); // "Constructed"
```

Since this constructor takes no arguments, the parentheses may optionally be left out.

```php
$r = new MyRectangle; // "Constructed"
```

Just as any other method, the constructor can have a parameter list. It can be used to set the property values to the arguments passed when the object is created.

```php
class MyRectangle
{
  public $x, $y;

  function __construct($x, $y)
  {
    $this->x = $x;
    $this->y = $y;
  }
}

$r = new MyRectangle(5,10);
```

Destructor

In addition to the constructor, classes can also have a destructor. This magic method starts with two underscores followed by the word destruct. It is called as soon as there are no more references to the object, before the object is destroyed by the PHP garbage collector.

```php
class MyRectangle
{
  // ...
  function __destruct() { echo "Destructed"; }
}
```

To test the destructor, the unset function can manually remove all references to the object.

```php
unset($r); // "Destructed"
```

Bear in mind that the object model was completely rewritten in PHP 5. Therefore, many features of classes, such as destructors, do not work in earlier versions of the language.

Case Sensitivity

Whereas variable names are case sensitive, class names in PHP are case insensitive—as are function names, keywords, and built-in constructs such as echo. This means that a class named MyClass can also be referenced as myclass or MYCLASS.

```php
class MyClass {}
$o1 = new myclass(); // ok
$o2 = new MYCLASS(); // ok
```

Object Comparison

When using the "equal to" operator (==) on objects, these objects are considered equal if the objects are instances of the same class and their properties have the same values and types. In contrast, the strict "equal to" operator (===) returns true only if the variables refer to the same instance of the same class.

```php
class Flag
{
  public $flag = true;
}
```

```
$a = new Flag();
$b = new Flag();

$c = ($a == $b);  // true (same values)
$d = ($a === $b); // false (different instances)
```

Anonymous Classes

Support for anonymous classes were introduced in PHP 7. Such a class is useful in place of a named class when only a single, throwaway object is needed.

```
$obj = new class {};
```

The implementation of the anonymous class, and the object created from it, are no different from a named class; for instance, they can use constructors in the same way as any named class.

```
$o = new class('Hi')
{
  public $x;
  public function __construct($a)
  {
    $this->x = $a;
  }
};

echo $o->x; // "Hi";
```

Closure Object

Anonymous functions in PHP are also closures, as they have the ability to capture a context from outside of the function's scope. In addition to variables, this context can also be an object's scope. This creates a so-called *closure object*, which has access to the properties of that object. An object closure is made using the bindTo method. This method accepts two arguments: the object to which the closure is bound and the class scope that it is associated with. To access non-public members (private or protected), the name of the class or object must be specified as the second argument.

```
class C { private $x = 'Hi'; }

$getC = function() { return $this->x; };
$getX = $getC->bindTo(new C, 'C');
echo $getX(); // "Hi"
```

This example uses two closures. The first closure, $getC, defines the method for retrieving the property. The second closure, $getX, is a duplicate of $getC, to which the object and class scope has been bound. PHP 7 simplified this by providing a shorthand—a better-performing way of temporarily binding and then calling a closure in the same operation.

```php
// PHP 7+ code
$getX = function() { return $this->x; };
echo $getX->call(new C); // "Hi"
```

CHAPTER 10

■ ■ ■

Inheritance

Inheritance allows a class to acquire the members of another class. In the following example, the Square class inherits from Rectangle, specified by the extends keyword. Rectangle then becomes the parent class of Square, which in turn becomes a child class of Rectangle. In addition to its own members, Square gains all accessible (non-private) members in Rectangle, including any constructor.

```php
// Parent class (base class)
class Rectangle
{
  public $x, $y;
  function __construct($a, $b)
  {
    $this->x = $a;
    $this->y = $b;
  }
}

// Child class (derived class)
class Square extends Rectangle {}
```

When creating an instance of Square, two arguments must now be specified because Square has inherited Rectangle's constructor.

```php
$s = new Square(5,10);
```

The properties inherited from Rectangle can also be accessed from the Square object.

```php
$s->x = 5; $s->y = 10;
```

A class in PHP may only inherit from one parent class and the parent must be defined before the child class in the script file.

© Mikael Olsson 2016
M. Olsson, *PHP 7 Quick Scripting Reference*, DOI 10.1007/978-1-4842-1922-5_10

Overriding Members

A member in a child class can redefine a member in its parent class to give it a new implementation. To override an inherited member, it just needs to be redeclared with the same name. As shown in the following, the Square constructor overrides the constructor in Rectangle.

```php
class Square extends Rectangle
{
  function __construct($a)
  {
    $this->x = $a;
    $this->y = $a;
  }
}
```

With this new constructor, only a single argument is used to create the Square.

```php
$s = new Square(5);
```

Because the inherited constructor of Rectangle is overridden, Rectangle's constructor is no longer called when the Square object is created. It is up to the developer to call the parent constructor, if necessary. This is done by prepending the call with the parent keyword and a double colon. The double colon is known as the *scope resolution operator* (::).

```php
class Square extends Rectangle
{
  function __construct($a)
  {
    parent::__construct($a,$a);
  }
}
```

The parent keyword is an alias for the parent's class name, which may alternatively be used. In PHP, it is possible to access overridden members that are any number of levels deep in the inheritance hierarchy using this notation.

```php
class Square extends Rectangle
{
  function __construct($a)
  {
    Rectangle::__construct($a,$a);
  }
}
```

Like constructors, the parent destructor is not called implicitly if it is overridden. It, too, would have to be explicitly called with parent::__destruct() from the child destructor.

Final Keyword

To stop a child class from overriding a method, it can be defined as final. A class itself can also be defined as final to prevent any class from extending it.

```
final class NotExtendable
{
  final function notOverridable() {}
}
```

Instanceof Operator

As a safety precaution, you can test to see whether an object can be cast to a specific class by using the instanceof operator. This operator returns true if the left side object can be cast into the right side type without causing an error. This is true when the object is an instance of, or inherits from, the right-side class.

```
$s = new Square(5);
$s instanceof Square;    // true
$s instanceof Rectangle; // true
```

CHAPTER 11

Access Levels

Every class member has an accessibility level that determines where the member is visible. There are three of them available in PHP: public, protected, and private.

```
class MyClass
{
  public    $myPublic;    // unrestricted access
  protected $myProtected; // enclosing or child class
  private   $myPrivate;   // enclosing class only
}
```

Private Access

All members, regardless of access level, are accessible in the class in which they are declared—the enclosing class. This is the only place where a private member can be accessed.

```
class MyClass
{
  public    $myPublic    = 'public';
  protected $myProtected = 'protected';
  private   $myPrivate   = 'private';

  function test()
  {
    echo $this->myPublic;    // allowed
    echo $this->myProtected; // allowed
    echo $this->myPrivate;   // allowed
  }
}
```

Unlike properties, methods do not have to have an explicit access level specified. They default to public access unless set to another level.

Protected Access

A protected member can be accessed from inside the child or the parent classes, as well as from within the enclosing class.

```
class MyChild extends MyClass
{
  function test()
  {
    echo $this->myPublic;    // allowed
    echo $this->myProtected; // allowed
    echo $this->myPrivate;   // inaccessible
  }
}
```

Public Access

Public members have unrestricted access. In addition to anywhere a protected member can be accessed, a public member can also be reached through an object variable.

```
$m = new MyClass();
echo $m->myPublic;    // allowed
echo $m->myProtected; // inaccessible
echo $m->myPrivate;   // inaccessible
```

Var Keyword

Before PHP 5, the var keyword was used to declare properties. To maintain backward compatibility, this keyword is still usable and gives public access, just like the public modifier.

```
class MyVars
{
  var $x, $y; // deprecated property declaration
}
```

Object Access

In PHP, objects of the same class have access to each other's private and protected members. This behavior is different from many other programming languages where such access is not allowed.

```
class MyClass
{
  private $myPrivate;

  function setPrivate($obj, $val) {
    $obj->myPrivate = $val; // set private property
  }
}
$a = new MyClass();
$b = new MyClass();
$a->setPrivate($b, 10);
```

Access Level Guideline

As a guideline, when choosing an access level, it is generally best to use the most restrictive level possible. This is because the more places a member can be accessed, the more places it can be accessed incorrectly, which makes the code harder to debug. Using restrictive access levels also makes it easier to modify the class without breaking the code for any other developers using that class.

CHAPTER 12

Static

The static keyword can be used to declare properties and methods that can be accessed without having to create an instance of the class. Static (class) members only exist in one copy, which belongs to the class itself, whereas instance (non-static) members are created as new copies for each new object.

```php
class MyCircle
{
  // Instance members (one per object)
  public $r = 10;
  function getArea() {}

  // Static/class members (only one copy)
  static $pi = 3.14;
  static function newArea($a) {}
}
```

Static methods cannot use instance members since these methods are not part of an instance. They can use other static members, however.

Referencing Static Members

Unlike instance members, static members are not accessed using the single arrow operator (->). Instead, to reference static members inside a class, the member must be prefixed with the self keyword followed by the scope resolution operator (::). The self keyword is an alias for the class name, so alternatively, the actual name of the class can be used.

```php
static function newArea($a)
{
  return self::$pi * $a * $a;      // ok
  return MyCircle::$pi * $a * $a; // alternative
}
```

© Mikael Olsson 2016
M. Olsson, *PHP 7 Quick Scripting Reference*, DOI 10.1007/978-1-4842-1922-5_12

This same syntax is used to access static members from an instance method. Note that in contrast to static methods, instance methods can use both static and instance members.

```
function getArea()
{
  return self::newArea($this->$r);
}
```

To access static members from outside the class, the name of the class needs to be used, followed by the scope resolution operator (::).

```
class MyCircle
{
  static $pi = 3.14;

  static function newArea($a)
  {
    return self::$pi * $a * $a;
  }
}

echo MyCircle::$pi; // "3.14"
echo MyCircle::newArea(10); // "314"
```

The advantage of static members can be seen here; they can be used without having to create an instance of the class. Therefore, methods should be declared static if they perform a generic function independently of instance variables. Likewise, properties should be declared static if there is only need for a single instance of the variable.

Static Variables

Local variables can be declared static to make the function remember its value. Such a static variable only exists in the local function's scope, but it does not lose its value when the function ends. This can be used to count the number of times a function is called, for example.

```
function add()
{
  static $val = 0;
  echo $val++;
}

add(); // "0"
add(); // "1"
add(); // "2"
```

The initial value that a static variable is given is only set once. Keep in mind that static properties and static variables may only be initialized with a constant; but not with an expression, such as another variable or a function return value.

Late Static Bindings

As mentioned before, the self keyword is an alias for the class name of the enclosing class. This means that the keyword refers to its enclosing class even when it is called from the context of a child class.

```
class MyParent
{
  protected static $val = 'parent';

  public static function getVal()
  {
    return self::$val;
  }
}

class MyChild extends MyParent
{
  protected static $val = 'child';
}

echo MyChild::getVal(); // "parent"
```

To get the class reference to evaluate to the actual calling class, the static keyword needs to be used instead of the self keyword. This feature is called *late static bindings* and it was added in PHP 5.3.

```
class MyParent
{
  protected static $val = 'parent';

  public static function getLateBindingVal()
  {
    return static::$val;
  }
}

class MyChild extends MyParent
{
  protected static $val = 'child';
}
echo MyChild::getLateBindingVal(); // "child"
```

CHAPTER 13

Constants

A *constant* is a variable with a value that cannot be changed by the script. Therefore, such a value must be assigned at the same time that the constant is created. PHP provides two methods for creating constants: the const modifier and the define function.

Const

The const modifier is used to create class constants. Unlike regular properties, class constants do not have an access level specified because they are always publicly visible. They also do not use the dollar sign parser token ($). The naming convention for constants is all uppercase, with underscores separating each word.

```
class MyCircle
{
  const PI = 3.14;
}
```

Constants must be assigned a value when they are created. Like static properties, a constant may only be initialized with a constant value, and not with an expression. Class constants are referenced in the same way as static properties, except that they do not use the dollar sign.

```
echo MyCircle::PI; // "3.14"
```

The const modifier may not be applied to local variables or parameters. However, as of PHP 5.3, const can be used to create global constants. Such a constant is defined in the global scope and can be accessed anywhere in the script.

```
const PI = 3.14;
echo PI; // "3.14"
```

Define

The define function can create both global and local constants, but not class constants. The first argument to this function is the constant's name and the second is its value.

```
define('DEBUG', 1);
```

Just like constants created with const, define constants are used without the dollar sign and their value cannot be modified.

```
echo DEBUG; // "1"
```

Like constants created with const, the value for define may be any scalar data type: integer, float, string, or bool. Unlike const, however, the define function allows an expression to be used in the assignment, such as a variable or the result of a mathematical expression.

```
define('ONE', 1);      // 1
define('TWO', ONE+1); // 2
```

Constants are case sensitive by default. However, the define function takes a third optional argument that may be set to true to create a case-insensitive constant.

```
define('DEBUG', 1, true);
echo debug; // "1"
```

To check whether a constant already exists, the defined function can be used. This function works for constants created with const or define.

```
if (!defined('PI'))
  define('PI', 3.14);
```

PHP 7 made it possible to create constant arrays using the define function. Support for constant arrays created with const has existed since PHP 5.6.

```
const CA = [1, 2, 3];    // PHP 5.6 or later
define('DA', [1, 2, 3]); // PHP 7 or later
```

Const and define

The const modifier creates a compile-time constant, so the compiler replaces all usage of the constant with its value. In contrast, define creates a run-time constant that is not set until run-time. This is the reason why define constants may be assigned with expressional values, whereas const requires constant values that are known at compile-time.

```
const PI = 3.14;    // compile-time constant
define('E', 2.72); // run-time constant
```

Only const may be used for class constants and only define for local constants. However, when creating global constants, both const and define are allowed. In these circumstances, using const is generally preferable, as compile-time constants are slightly faster than run-time constants. The main exception is when the constant is conditionally defined, or an expressional value is required, in which case define must be used.

Constant Guideline

In general, it is a good idea to create constants instead of variables if their values do not need to be changed. This ensures that the variables are not changed anywhere in the script by mistake, which in turn helps to prevent bugs.

Magic Constants

PHP provides eight predefined constants, as shown in Table 13-1. These are called *magic constants* because their values change, depending on where they are used.

Table 13-1. *Magic Constants*

Name	Description
__LINE__	Current line number of the file.
__FILE__	Full path and filename of the file.
__DIR__	Directory of the file.
__FUNCTION__	Function name.
__CLASS__	Class name including namespace.
__TRAIT__	Trait name including namespace.
__METHOD__	Class method name.
__NAMESPACE__	Current namespace.

Magic constants are especially useful for debugging purposes. For example, the value of __LINE__ depends on the line in which it appears in the script.

```
if(!isset($var))
{
  echo '$var not set on line ' . __LINE__;
}
```

CHAPTER 14

Interface

An interface specifies methods that classes using the interface must implement. They are defined with the `interface` keyword, followed by a name and a code block. Their naming convention is to start with a small i and then to have each word initially capitalized.

```
interface iMyInterface {}
```

Interface Signatures

The code block for an interface can contain signatures for instance methods. These methods cannot have any implementations. Instead, their bodies are replaced by semicolons. Interface methods must always be public.

```
interface iMyInterface
{
  public function myMethod();
}
```

Additionally, interfaces may define constants. These interface constants behave just as class constants, except that they cannot be overridden.

```
interface iMyInterface
{
  const PI = 3.14;
}
```

An interface may not inherit from a class, but it may inherit from another interface, which effectively combines the interfaces into one.

```
interface i1 {}
interface i2 extends i1 {}
```

© Mikael Olsson 2016
M. Olsson, *PHP 7 Quick Scripting Reference*, DOI 10.1007/978-1-4842-1922-5_14

Interface Example

The following example shows an interface called iComparable, which has a single method named Compare. Note that this method makes use of type hinting to make sure that the method is called with the correct type. This functionality is covered in a later chapter.

```
interface iComparable
{
  public function compare(iComparable $o);
}
```

The Circle class implements this interface by using the implements keyword after the class name, followed by the interface name. If the class also has an extends clause, the implements clause needs to be placed after it. Bear in mind that although a class can only inherit from one parent class, it may implement any number of interfaces by specifying them in a comma-separated list.

```
class Circle implements iComparable
{
  public $r;
}
```

Because Circle implements iComparable, it must define the compare() method. For this class, the method returns the difference between the circle radiuses. The implemented method must be public, in addition to having the same signature as the method defined in the interface. It may also have more parameters, as long as they are optional.

```
class Circle implements iComparable
{
  public $r;

  public function compare(iComparable $o)
  {
    return $this->r - $o->r;
  }
}
```

Interface Usages

Interfaces allow for multiple inheritance of class design without the complications associated with allowing multiple inheritance of functionality. The main benefit of requiring a specific class design can be seen with the iComparable interface, which defines a specific functionality that classes can share. It allows developers to use interface members without having to know the actual type of a class. To illustrate, the following example shows a simple method that takes two iComparable objects and returns the largest one.

```
function largest(iComparable $a, iComparable $b)
{
  return ($a->compare($b) > 0) ? $a : $b;
}
```

This method works for any two objects of the same type that implement the iComparable interface. It works regardless of what type the objects are since the method only uses the functionality exposed through that interface.

Interface Guideline

An interface provides a design for a class without any implementation. It is a contract by which classes that implement it agree to provide certain functionality. This has two benefits. First, it provides a way to make sure that developers implement certain methods. Second, because these classes are guaranteed to have certain methods, they can be used even without knowing the class's actual type, which allows the code to be more flexible.

CHAPTER 15

Abstract

An abstract class provides a partial implementation that other classes can build upon. When a class is declared as abstract, it means that the class can contain incomplete methods that must be implemented in child classes, in addition to normal class members.

Abstract Methods

In an abstract class, any method can be declared abstract. These methods are then left unimplemented and only their signatures are specified, while their code blocks are replaced by semicolons.

```
abstract class Shape
{
  abstract public function myAbstract();
}
```

Abstract Example

To give an example, the following class has two properties and an abstract method.

```
abstract class Shape
{
  private $x = 100, $y = 100;
  abstract public function getArea();
}
```

If a class inherits from this abstract class, it is then forced to override the abstract method. The method signature must match, except for the access level, which can be made less restricted.

```
class Rectangle extends Shape

{
  public function getArea()
  {
    return $this->x * $this->y;
  }
}
```

It is not possible to instantiate an abstract class. They serve only as parents for other classes, partly dictating their implementation.

```
$s = new Shape(); // compile-time error
```

However, an abstract class may inherit from a non-abstract (concrete) class.

```
class NonAbstract {}
abstract class MyAbstract extends NonAbstract {}
```

Abstract Classes and Interfaces

Abstract classes are in many ways similar to interfaces. They can both define member signatures that the deriving classes must implement, and neither one of them can be instantiated. The key differences are, first, that the abstract class can contain non-abstract members, while the interface cannot. Second, a class can implement any number of interfaces but only inherit from one class, abstract or not.

```
// Defines default functionality and definitions
abstract class Shape
{
  public $x = 100, $y = 100;
  abstract public function getArea();
}
// Class is a Shape
class Rectangle extends Shape { /*...*/ }

// Defines a specific functionality
interface iComparable
{
  function compare();
}
// Class can be compared
class MyClass implements iComparable { /*...*/ }
```

Abstract Guideline

An abstract class provides a partially implemented base class that dictates how child classes must behave. They are most useful when child classes share some similarities, but differ in other implementations that child classes are required to define. Just like interfaces, abstract classes are useful constructs in object-oriented programming that help developers follow good coding standards.

CHAPTER 16

Traits

A *trait* is a group of methods that can be inserted into classes. They were added in PHP 5.4 to enable greater code reuse without the added complexity that comes from allowing multiple inheritance. Traits are defined with the trait keyword, followed by a name and a code block. The naming convention is the same as for classes, with each word initially capitalized. The code block may only contain static and instance methods.

```
trait PrintFunctionality
{
  public function myPrint() { echo 'Hello'; }
}
```

Classes that need the functionality that a trait provides can include it with the use keyword, followed by the trait's name. The trait's methods then behave as if they were directly defined in that class.

```
class MyClass
{
  // Insert trait methods
  use PrintFunctionality;
}

$o = new MyClass();
$o->myPrint(); // "Hello"
```

A class may use multiple traits by placing them in a comma-separated list. Similarly, a trait may be composed from one or more other traits.

Inheritance and Traits

Trait methods override inherited methods. Likewise, methods defined in the class override methods inserted by a trait.

```
class MyParent
{
  public function myPrint() { echo 'Base'; }
}

class MyChild extends MyParent
{
  // Overrides inherited method
  use PrintFunctionality;
  // Overrides trait inserted method
  public function myPrint() { echo 'Child'; }
}

$o = new MyChild();
$o->myPrint(); // "Child"
```

Trait Guidelines

Single inheritance sometimes forces the developer to make a choice between code reuse and a conceptually clean class hierarchy. To achieve greater code reuse, methods can be moved near the root of the class hierarchy, but then classes start to have methods that they do not need, which reduces the understandability and maintainability of the code. On the other hand, enforcing conceptual cleanliness in the class hierarchy often leads to code duplication, which may cause inconsistencies. Traits provide a way to avoid this shortcoming with single inheritance, which enables code reuse that is independent of the class hierarchy.

CHAPTER 17

■ ■ ■

Importing Files

The same code often needs to be called on multiple pages. This can be done by first placing the code inside a separate file and then including that file using the `include` statement. This statement takes all the text in the specified file and includes it in the script, as if the code had been copied to that location. Just like `echo`, `include` is a special language construct and not a function, so parentheses should not be used.

```php
<?php
include 'myfile.php';
?>
```

When a file is included, parsing changes to HTML mode at the beginning of the target file and resumes PHP mode again at the end. For this reason, any code inside the included file that needs to be executed as PHP code must be enclosed within PHP tags.

```php
<?php
// myfile.php
?>
```

Include Path

An include file can either be specified with a relative path, an absolute path, or without a path. A *relative file path* is relative to the importing file's directory. An *absolute file path* includes the full file path.

```php
// Relative path
include 'myfolder\myfile.php';

// Absolute path
include 'C:\xampp\htdocs\myfile.php';
```

When a relative path or no path is specified, include first searches for the file in the current working directory, which defaults to the directory of the importing script. If the file is not found there, include checks the folders specified by the include_path[1] directive defined in php.ini before failing.

```
// No path
include 'myfile.php';
```

In addition to include, there are three other language constructs available for importing the content of one file into another: require, include_once, and require_once.

Require

The require construct includes and evaluates the specified file. It is identical to include, except in how it handles failure. When a file import fails, require halts the script with an error; whereas include only issues a warning. An import may fail either because the file is not found or because the user running the web server does not have read access to it.

```
require 'myfile.php'; // halt on error
```

Generally, it is best to use require for any complex PHP application or CMS site. That way, the application does not attempt to run when a key file is missing. For less critical code segments and simple PHP web sites, include may suffice, in which case PHP shows the output, even if the included file is missing.

Include_once

The include_once statement behaves like include, except that if the specified file has already been included, it is not included again.

```
include_once 'myfile.php'; // include only once
```

Require_once

The require_once statement works like require, but it does not import a file if it has already been imported.

```
require_once 'myfile.php'; // require only once
```

---

[1]http://www.php.net/manual/en/ini.core.php#ini.include-path

The include_once and require_once statements may be used instead of include and require in cases, where the same file might be imported more than once during a particular execution of a script. This avoids errors caused by function and class redefinitions, for example.

Return

It is possible to execute a return statement inside an imported file. This stops the execution and returns to the script that called the file import.

```php
<?php
// myimport.php
return 'OK';
?>
```

If a return value is specified, the import statement evaluates to that value, just like a normal function.

```php
<?php
// myfile.php
if ((include 'myimport.php') == 'OK')
  echo 'OK';
?>
```

_Autoload

For large web applications, the number of includes required in every script may be substantial. This can be avoided by defining an __autoload function. This function is automatically invoked when an undefined class or interface is used to try to load that definition. It takes one parameter, which is the name of the class or interface that PHP is looking for.

```php
function __autoload($class_name)
{
  include $class_name . '.php';
}

// Attempt to auto include MyClass.php
$obj = new MyClass();
```

A good coding practice to follow when writing object-oriented applications is to have one source file for every class definition, and to name the file according to the class name. Following this convention, the __autoload function is able to load the class—provided that it is in the same folder as the script file that needed it.

```php
<?php
// myclass.php
class MyClass {}
?>
```

If the file is located in a subfolder, the class name can include underscore characters to symbolize this. The underscore characters then need to be converted into directory separators in the __autoload function.

CHAPTER 18

Type Declarations

Type declarations allow a function to declare the expected types of their parameters and return value. This permits the PHP engine to enforce that the specified types are used.

Argument Type Declarations

Early versions of PHP relied exclusively on proper documentation of functions for developers to know what arguments a function accepts. To allow for functions that are more robust, PHP 5 began to introduce *argument type declarations*, permitting the type of a function parameter to be specified. Valid types for type declarations are shown in Table 18-1, along with the PHP version in which these types were added.

Table 18-1. *Type Declarations*

Name	Description	Version
class name	Argument must be an object or a child of this class.	PHP 5.0
interface name	Argument must be an object implementing this interface.	PHP 5.0
array	Argument must be an array.	PHP 5.1
callable	Argument must be callable as a function.	PHP 5.4
bool	Argument must be a Boolean value.	PHP 7.0
float	Argument must be a floating-point number.	PHP 7.0
int	Argument must be an integer.	PHP 7.0
string	Argument must be a string.	PHP 7.0

A type declaration is set by prefixing the parameter with the type in the function signature. The following is an example using the array pseudo type introduced in PHP 5.1.

© Mikael Olsson 2016
M. Olsson, *PHP 7 Quick Scripting Reference*, DOI 10.1007/978-1-4842-1922-5_18

```
function myPrint(array $a)
{
  foreach ($a as $v) { echo $v; }
}

myPrint( array(1,2,3) ); // "123"
```

Failing to satisfy the type hint results in a fatal error. This gives a quick way for the developer to detect when an invalid argument is used.

```
myPrint('Test'); // error
```

The callable pseudo type was added in PHP 5.4. With this type hint in place, the argument must be a callable function, method, or object. Language constructs such as echo are not allowed, but anonymous functions may be used, as in the following example.

```
function myCall(callable $callback, $data)
{
  $callback($data);
}

$say = function($s) { echo $s; };
myCall( $say, 'Hi' ); // "Hi";
```

To pass a method as a callback function, both the object and the method name need to be grouped together as an array.

```
class MyClass {
  function myCallback($s) {
    echo $s;
  }
}

$o = new MyClass();
myCall( array($o, 'myCallback'), 'Hi' ); // "Hi"
```

Type declarations for scalar types—including bool, int, float, and string—were added in PHP 7. The following is a simple example using the bool type.

```
function isTrue(bool $b)
{
  return ($b === true);
}

echo isTrue(true);  // "1"
echo isTrue(false); // ""
```

It is a good idea to use type declarations for functions that rely on an argument being of a specific type. That way, if this function is mistakenly passed an argument of the incorrect type, it immediately triggers an error. Without a type declaration, the function may fail silently, making the error that much more difficult to detect.

Return Type Declarations

Support for return type declarations was added in PHP 7 as a way to prevent unintended return values. The return type is declared after the parameter list. The same types are allowed as for argument type declarations.

```
function f(): array {
  return [];
}
```

When used with an interface, type declarations force implementing classes to match the same type declarations.

```
interface I {
  static function myArray(array $a): array;
}

class C implements I {
  static function myArray(array $a): array {
    return $a;
  }
}
```

Strict Typing

The default behavior in PHP is to attempt to convert scalar values of incorrect type into the expected type. For instance, a function expecting a string can still be called with an integer argument, because an integer can be converted into a string.

```
function showString(string $s) {
  echo $s;
}

showString(5); // "5"
```

77

Strong type checking can be enabled in a specific source file by placing the following declaration as the first statement in that file.

```
declare(strict_types=1);
```

This affects both argument and return type declarations of scalar type, which must then be of the exact type declared in the function.

```
showString(5); // Fatal error: Uncaught TypeError
```

CHAPTER 19

Type Conversions

PHP automatically converts a variable's data type as necessary, given the context in which it is used. For this reason, explicit type conversions are seldom required. Nonetheless, the type of a variable or expression may be changed by performing an explicit type cast.

Explicit Casts

An explicit cast is performed by placing the desired data type in parentheses before the variable or value that is to be evaluated. In the following example, the explicit cast forces the bool variable to be evaluated as an int.

```
$myBool = false;
$myInt = (int)$myBool; // 0
```

One use for explicit casts can be seen when the bool variable is sent as output to the page. Due to automatic type conversions, the false value becomes an empty string; therefore, it is not displayed. By first converting it to an integer, the false value shows up as 0 instead.

```
echo $myBool;       // ""
echo (int)$myBool; // "0"
```

Allowed casts are listed in Table 19-1.

Table 19-1. *Allowed Type Casts*

Name	Description
(int), (integer)	Cast to int
(bool), (boolean)	Cast to bool
(float), (double), (real)	Cast to float
(string)	Cast to string
(array)	Cast to array
(object)	Cast to object
(unset)	Cast to null

© Mikael Olsson 2016
M. Olsson, *PHP 7 Quick Scripting Reference*, DOI 10.1007/978-1-4842-1922-5_19

To give some examples, the array cast converts a scalar type to an array with a single element. It performs the same function as using the array constructor.

```
$myInt = 10;
$myArr = (array)$myInt;
$myArr = array($myInt); // same as above
echo $myArr[0]; // "10"
```

If a scalar type such as int is cast to object, it becomes an instance of the built-in stdClass class. The value of the variable is stored in a property of this class, called scalar.

```
$myObj = (object)$myInt;
echo $myObj->scalar; // "10"
```

The unset cast makes the variable evaluate to null. Despite its name, it does not actually unset the variable. The cast merely exists for the sake of completeness, because null is considered a data type.

```
$myNull = (unset)$myInt;
$myNull = null; // same as above
```

Settype

An explicit cast does not change the type of the variable it precedes, only how it is evaluated in that expression. To change the type of a variable, the settype function can be used, which takes two arguments. The first is the variable to be converted and the second is the data type given as a string.

```
$myVar = 1.2;
settype($myVar, 'int'); // convert variable to int
```

Alternatively, a type conversion can be performed by storing the result of an explicit cast back into the same variable.

```
$myVar = 1.2;
$myVar = (int)$myVar; // 1
```

Gettype

Related to settype is the gettype function, which returns the type of the supplied argument as a human-readable string.

```
$myBool = true;
echo gettype($myBool); // "boolean"
```

CHAPTER 20

Variable Testing

As a web-focused language, it is common in PHP to process user-supplied data. Such data needs to be tested before it is used to confirm that it exists and has a valid value. PHP provides a number of built-in constructs that can be used for this purpose.

Isset

The isset language construct returns true if the variable exists and has been assigned a value other than null.

```
isset($a); // false

$a = 10;
isset($a); // true

$a = null;
isset($a); // false
```

Empty

The empty construct checks whether the specified variable has an empty value— such as null, 0, false, or an empty string—and returns true if that is the case. It also returns true if the variable does not exist.

```
empty($b); // true

$b = false;
empty($b); // true
```

© Mikael Olsson 2016
M. Olsson, *PHP 7 Quick Scripting Reference*, DOI 10.1007/978-1-4842-1922-5_20

Is_null

The is_null construct can be used to test whether a variable is set to null.

```
$c = null;
is_null($c); // true

$c = 10;
is_null($c); // false
```

If the variable does not exist, is_null also returns true, but with an error notice because it is not supposed to be used with uninitialized variables.

```
is_null($d); // true (undefined variable notice)
```

A strict equality check against null is functionally equivalent to using the is_null construct. Using this operator instead is often preferred because it is more readable and marginally faster, as it does not involve a function call overhead.

```
$c = null;
$c === null; // true
```

Unset

Another language construct that is useful to know about is unset, which deletes a variable from the current scope.

```
$e = 10;
unset($e); // delete $e
```

When a global variable is made accessible in a function with the global keyword, this code actually creates a local reference to the global variable in the $GLOBALS array. For this reason, attempting to unset a global variable in a function only deletes the local reference. To delete the global variable from a function's scope, the unset has to be made directly on the $GLOBALS array.

```
function myUnset()
{
  // Make $o a reference to $GLOBALS['o']
  global $o;

  // Remove the reference variable
  unset($o);

  // Remove the global variable
  unset($GLOBALS['o']);
}
```

Unsetting a variable is slightly different from setting the variable to null. When a variable is set to null, the variable still exists, but the variable content it held is immediately freed. In contrast, unsetting a variable deletes the variable, but the memory is still considered to be in use until the garbage collector clears it. Performance issues aside, using unset is recommended because it makes the code's intent clearer.

```
$var = null; // free memory
unset($var); // delete variable
```

Keep in mind that, most of the time, it is not necessary to manually unset variables, because the PHP garbage collector automatically deletes variables when they go out of scope. However, if a server performs memory-intensive tasks, then unsetting those variables manually allows the server to handle a greater number of simultaneous requests before running out of memory.

Null Coalescing Operator

The null coalescing operator (??) was added in PHP 7 as a shortcut for the common case of using a ternary with isset. It returns its first operand if it exists and is not null; otherwise, it returns its second operand.

```
$x = null;
$name = $x ?? 'unknown'; // "unknown"
```

This statement is equivalent to the following ternary operation, which uses the isset construct.

```
$name = isset($x) ? $x : 'unknown';
```

Determining Types

PHP has several useful functions for determining the type of a variable. These functions can be seen in Table 20-1.

Table 20-1. *Functions for Determining the Type of a Variable*

Name	Description
is_array()	True if variable is an array.
is_bool()	True if variable is a bool.
is_callable()	True if variable can be called as a function.
is_float(), is_double(), is_real()	True if variable is a float.
is_int(), is_integer(), is_long()	True if variable is an integer.
is_null()	True if variable is set to null.
is_numeric()	True if variable is a number or numeric string.
is_scalar()	True if variable is an int, float, string, or bool.
is_object()	True if variable is an object.
is_resource()	True if variable is a resource.
is_string()	True if variable is a string.

To give an example, the is_numeric function returns true if the argument contains either a number or a string that can be evaluated to a number.

```
is_numeric(10.5);    // true   (float)
is_numeric('33');    // true   (numeric string)
is_numeric('text');  // false  (non-numeric string)
```

Variable Information

PHP has three built-in functions for retrieving information about variables: print_r, var_dump, and var_export. The print_r function displays the value of a variable in a human-readable way. It is useful for debugging purposes.

```
$a = array('one', 'two', 'three');
print_r($a);
```

The preceding code produces the following output.

```
Array ( [0] => one [1] => two [2] => three )
```

Similar to `print_r` is `var_dump`, which in addition to values, also displays data types and sizes. Calling `var_dump($a)` shows this output.

```
array(3) {
  [0]=> string(3) "one"
  [1]=> string(3) "two"
  [2]=> string(5) "three"
}
```

Finally, there is the `var_export` function, which prints variable information in a style that can be used as PHP code. The following shows the output for `var_export($a)`. Note the trailing comma after the last element, which is allowed.

```
array ( 0 => 'one', 1 => 'two', 2 => 'three', )
```

The `var_export` function, along with `print_r`, accepts an optional Boolean second argument. When set to `true`, the function returns the output instead of printing it. This gives `var_export` further uses, such as being combined with the `eval` language construct. This construct takes a string argument and evaluates it as PHP code.

```
eval('$b = ' . var_export($a, true) . ';');
```

The ability to execute arbitrary code with `eval` is a powerful feature that should be used with care. It should not be used to execute any user-provided data, at least not without proper validation, as this represents a security risk. Another reason why the use of `eval` is discouraged is because similar to `goto`, it makes the execution of code more difficult to follow, which complicates debugging.

CHAPTER 21

Overloading

Overloading in PHP provides the ability to add object members at run-time. This is done by having the class implement the overloading methods __get, __set, __call, and __callStatic. Bear in mind that the meaning of overloading in PHP is different from many other languages.

Property Overloading

The __get and __set methods provide a convenient way to implement getter and setter methods, which are methods that are often used to safely read and write to properties. These overloading methods are invoked when using properties that are inaccessible, either because they are not defined in the class or because they are unavailable from the current scope. In the following example, the __set method adds any inaccessible properties to the $data array, and __get safely retrieves the elements.

```php
class MyProperties
{
  private $data = array();

  public function __set($name, $value)
  {
    $this->data[$name] = $value;
  }

  public function __get($name)
  {
    if (array_key_exists($name, $this->data))
      return $this->data[$name];
  }
}
```

When setting the value of an inaccessible property, __set is called with the name of the property and the value as its arguments. Similarly, when accessing an inaccessible property, __get is called with the property name as its argument.

```
$obj = new MyProperties();

$obj->a = 1;  // __set called
echo $obj->a; // __get called
```

Method Overloading

There are two methods for handling calls to inaccessible methods of a class: __call and __callStatic. The __call method is invoked for instance method calls.

```
class MyClass
{
  public function __call($name, $args)
  {
    echo "Calling $name $args[0]";
  }
}

// "Calling myTest in object context"
(new MyClass())->myTest('in object context');
```

The first argument to __call is the name of the method being called and the second is a numeric array containing the parameters passed to the method. These arguments are the same for the __callStatic method, which handles calls to inaccessible static methods.

```
class MyClass
{
  public static function __callStatic($name, $args)
  {
    echo "Calling $name $args[0]";
  }
}

// "Calling myTest in static context"
MyClass::myTest('in static context');
```

Isset and unset Overloading

The built-in constructs isset, empty, and unset only work on explicitly defined properties, not overloaded ones. This functionality is added to a class by overloading the __isset and __unset methods.

```php
class MyClass
{
  private $data = array();

  public function __set($name, $value) {
    $this->data[$name] = $value;
  }
  public function __get($name) {
    if (array_key_exists($name, $this->data))
      return $this->data[$name];
  }

  public function __isset($name) {
    return isset($this->data[$name]);
  }

  public function __unset($name) {
    unset( $this->data[$name] );
  }
}
```

The __isset method is invoked when isset is called on an inaccessible property.

```php
$obj = new MyClass();
$obj->name = "Joe";

isset($obj->name); // true
isset($obj->age);  // false
```

When unset is called on an inaccessible property, the __unset method handles that call.

```php
unset($obj->name); // delete property
isset($obj->name); // false
```

The empty construct only works on overloaded properties if both __isset and __get are implemented. If the result from __isset is false, the empty construct returns true. If, on the other hand, __isset returns true, then empty retrieves the property with __get and evaluates if it has a value considered to be empty.

```php
empty($obj->name); // false
empty($obj->age);  // true
```

CHAPTER 22

Magic Methods

There are a number of methods that can be implemented in a class for the purpose of being called internally by the PHP engine. These are known as *magic methods* and they are easy to recognize because they all start with two underscores. Table 22-1 lists the magic methods that have been discussed so far.

Table 22-1. Magic Methods

Name	Description
__construct(...)	Called when creating a new instance.
__destruct()	Called when object has no references left.
__call($name, $array)	Called when invoking inaccessible methods in an object context.
__callStatic($name, $array)	Called when invoking inaccessible methods in a static context.
__get($name)	Called when reading data from inaccessible properties.
__set($name, $value)	Called when writing data to inaccessible properties.
__isset($string)	Called when isset or empty is used on inaccessible properties.
__unset($string)	Called when unset is used on inaccessible properties.

In addition to these, there are six more magic methods that, like the others, can be implemented in classes to provide certain functionalities.

Table 22-2. *More Magic Methods*

Name	Description
__toString()	Called for object to string conversions.
__invoke(...)	Called for object to function conversions.
__sleep()	Called by serialize. Performs cleanup tasks and returns an array of variables to be serialized.
__wakeup()	Called by unserialize to reconstruct the object.
__set_state($array)	Called by var_export. The method must be static and its argument contains the exported properties.
__clone()	Called after object has been cloned.

__ToString

When an object is used in a context where a string is expected, the PHP engine searches for a method named __toString to retrieve a string representation of the object.

```
class MyClass
{
  public function __toString()
  {
    return 'Instance of ' . __CLASS__;
  }
}

$obj = new MyClass();
echo $obj; // "Instance of MyClass"
```

It is not possible to define how an object will behave when evaluated as types other than string.

_Invoke

The __invoke method allows an object to be treated as a function. Arguments provided when the object is called are used as the __invoke function's arguments.

```
class MyClass
{
  public function __invoke($arg)
  {
    echo $arg;
  }
}

$obj = new MyClass();
$obj('Test'); // "Test"
```

Object Serialization

Serialization is the process of converting data into a string format. This is useful for storing objects in databases or files. In PHP, the built-in serialize function performs this object-to-string conversion and unserialize converts the string back into the original object. The serialize function handles all types, except for the resource type, which is used to hold database connections and file handlers, for example. Consider the following simple database class.

```
class MyConnection
{
  public $link, $server, $user, $pass;

  public function connect()
  {
    $this->link = mysql_connect($this->server,
                                $this->user,
                                $this->pass);
  }
}
```

When this class is serialized, the database connection is lost and the $link resource type variable holding the connection is stored as null.

```
$obj = new MyConnection();
// ...

$bin = serialize($obj);    // serialize object
$obj = unserialize($bin); // restore object
```

To get greater control over how object data is serialized and unserialized, the __sleep and __wakeup methods may be implemented by this class.

93

_Sleep

The __sleep method is called by `serialize` and needs to return an array containing the properties that will be serialized. This array must not include private or protected properties because `serialize` is not able to access them. The method may also perform cleanup tasks before the serialization occurs, such as committing any pending data to storage mediums.

```
public function __sleep()
{
  return array('server', 'user', 'pass');
}
```

Note that the properties are returned to `serialize` in string form. The $link resource type pointer is not included in the array because it cannot be serialized. To reestablish the database connection, the __wakeup method can be used.

_Wakeup

Calling `unserialize` on the serialized object invokes the __wakeup method in order to restore the object. It accepts no arguments and does not need to return any value. It is used for reestablishing resource-type variables and for performing other initializing tasks that may need to be done after the object has been unserialized. In this example, it reestablishes the MySQL database connection.

```
public function __wakeup()
{
  if(isset($this->server, $this->user, $this->$pass))
    $this->connect();
}
```

Note that the `isset` construct is called here with multiple arguments, in which case it only returns `true` if all parameters are set.

Set State

The `var_export` function retrieves variable information that is usable as valid PHP code. In the following example, this function is used on an object.

```
class Fruit
{
  public $name = 'Lemon';
}

$export = var_export(new Fruit(), true);
```

Since an object is a complex type, there is no generic syntax for constructing it along with its members. Instead, var_export creates the following string.

```
Fruit::__set_state(array( 'name' => 'Lemon', ))
```

In order to construct it, this string relies on a static __set_state method being defined for the object. As shown, the __set_state method takes an associative array containing key-value pairs of each of the object's properties, including private and protected members.

```
static function __set_state(array $array)
{
  $tmp = new Fruit();
  $tmp->name = $array['name'];
  return $tmp;
}
```

With this method defined in the Fruit class, the exported string can now be parsed with the eval construct to create an identical object.

```
eval('$MyFruit = ' . $export . ';');
```

Object Cloning

Assigning an object to a variable only creates a new reference to the same object. To copy an object, the clone operator can be used.

```
class Fruit {}


$f1 = new Fruit();
$f2 = $f1;       // copy object reference
$f3 = clone $f1; // copy object
```

When an object is cloned, its properties are copied over to the new object. However, any child objects it may contain are not cloned, so they are shared between the copies. This is where the __clone method comes in. It is called on the cloned copy after the cloning is done. It can be used to clone any child objects.

```
class Apple {}

class FruitBasket
{
  public $apple;
```

```
    function __construct() { $apple = new Apple(); }

    function __clone()
    {
      $this->apple = clone $this->apple;
    }
}
```

CHAPTER 23

User Input

When an HTML form is submitted to a PHP page, the data becomes available to that script.

HTML Form

An HTML form has two required attributes: action and method. The action attribute specifies the script to which the form data is passed. For example, the following form submits one input property called myString to the mypage.php script file.

```
<!doctype html>
<html>
<body>
  <form action="mypage.php" method="post">
    <input type="text" name="myString">
    <input type="submit">
  </form>
</body>
</html>
```

The other required attribute of the form element specifies the sending method, which may be either GET or POST.

Sending with POST

If the form is sent using the POST method, the data is available through the $_POST array. The names of the properties are the keys in that associative array. Data sent with the POST method is not visible on the URL of the page, but this also means that the state of the page cannot be saved by, for example, bookmarking the page.

```
echo $_POST['myString'];
```

© Mikael Olsson 2016
M. Olsson, *PHP 7 Quick Scripting Reference*, DOI 10.1007/978-1-4842-1922-5_23

Sending with GET

The alternative to POST is to send the form data with the GET method and to retrieve it using the $_GET array. The variables are then displayed in the address bar, which effectively maintains the state of the page if it is bookmarked and revisited.

```
echo $_GET['myString'];
```

Because the data is contained in the address bar, variables cannot only be passed through HTML forms but also through HTML links. The $_GET array can then be used to change the state of the page accordingly. This provides one way of passing variables from one page to another.

```
<a href="mypage.php?myString=Foo+Bar">link</a>
```

Request Array

If it does not matter whether the POST or GET method was used to send the data, the $_REQUEST array can be used. This array typically contains the $_GET and $_POST arrays, but may also contain the $_COOKIE array.

```
echo $_REQUEST['myString']; // "Foo Bar"
```

The content of the $_REQUEST array can be set in the PHP configuration file[1] and varies between PHP distributions. Due to security concerns, the $_COOKIE array is usually not included.

Security Concerns

Any user-provided data can be manipulated; therefore, it should be validated and sanitized before being used. *Validation* means that you make sure that the data is in the form you expect, in terms of data type, range, and content. For example, the following code validates an email address.

```
if(!filter_var($_POST['email'], FILTER_VALIDATE_EMAIL))
  echo "Invalid email address";
```

Sanitizing is when you disable potentially malicious code in the user input. This is done by escaping the code according to the rules of the language where the input is to be used. For example, if the data is sent to a database, it needs to be sanitized with the mysql_real_escape_string function to disable any embedded SQL code.

---

[1]http://www.php.net/manual/en/ini.core.php#ini.request-order

```
// Sanitize for database use
$name = mysql_real_escape_string($_POST['name']);

// Execute SQL command
$sql = "SELECT * FROM users WHERE user='" . $name . "'";
$result = mysql_query($sql);
```

When user-supplied data is output to the web page as text, the htmlspecialchars function should be used. It disables any HTML markup, so that the user input is displayed but not interpreted.

```
// Sanitize for web page use
echo htmlspecialchars($_POST['comment']);
```

Submitting Arrays

Form data can be grouped into arrays by including array square brackets after the variable names in the form. This works for all form input elements, including <input>, <select>, and <textarea>.

```
<input type="text" name="myArr[]">
<input type="text" name="myArr[]">
```

The elements may also be assigned their own array keys.

```
<input type="text" name="myArr[name]">
```

Once submitted, the array is available for use in the script.

```
$val1 = $_POST['myArr'][0];
$val2 = $_POST['myArr'][1];
$name = $_POST['myArr']['name'];
```

The form <select> element has an attribute for allowing multiple items to be selected from the list.

```
<select name="myArr[]" size="3" multiple="true">
  <option value="apple">Apple</option>
  <option value="orange">Orange</option>
  <option value="pear">Pear</option>
</select>
```

When this multi-select element is included in a form, the array brackets become necessary for retrieving the selected values in the script.

```
foreach ($_POST['myArr'] as $item)
  echo $item . ' '; // ex "apple orange pear"
```

File Uploading

The HTML form provides a file input type that allows files to be uploaded to the server. For file uploading to work, the form's optional enctype attribute must be set to "multipart/form-data", as shown in the following example.

```
<form action="mypage.php" method="post"
      enctype="multipart/form-data">
  <input name="myfile" type="file">
  <input type="submit" value="Upload">
</form>
```

Information about the uploaded file is stored in the $_FILES array. The keys of this associative array are seen in Table 23-1.

Table 23-1. *Keys of the $_FILES Array*

Name	Description
name	Original name of uploaded file.
tmp_name	Path to temporary server copy.
type	Mime type of the file.
size	File size in bytes.
error	Error code.

A received file is only temporarily stored on the server. If it is not saved by the script, it will be deleted. The following shows a simple example of how to save the file. The example checks the error code to make sure that the file was successfully received, and if so, moves the file out of the temporary folder to save it. In practice, you would also want to examine the file size and type to determine whether the file is to be kept.

```
$dest = 'upload\\' . basename($_FILES['myfile']['name']);
$file = $_FILES['myfile']['tmp_name'];
$err  = $_FILES['myfile']['error'];

if($err == 0 && move_uploaded_file($file, $dest))
  echo 'File successfully uploaded';
```

Two new functions are seen in this example. The move_uploaded_file function checks to ensure that the first argument contains a valid upload file, and if so, it moves it to the path and renames it to the file name specified by the second argument. The specified folder must already exist, and if the function succeeds in moving the file, it returns true. The other new function is basename. It returns the file name component of a path, including the file extension.

Superglobals

As seen in this chapter, there are a number of built-in associative arrays that make external data available to PHP scripts. These arrays are known as *superglobals*, because they are automatically available in every scope. There are nine superglobals in PHP, each of which is described briefly in Table 23-2.

Table 23-2. *Superglobals*

Name	Description
$GLOBALS	Contains all global variables, including other superglobals.
$_GET	Contains variables sent via an HTTP GET request.
$_POST	Contains variables sent via an HTTP POST request.
$_FILES	Contains variables sent via an HTTP POST file upload.
$_COOKIE	Contains variables sent via HTTP cookies.
$_SESSION	Contains variables stored in a user's session.
$_REQUEST	Contains $_GET, $_POST, and possibly $_COOKIE variables.
$_SERVER	Contains information about the web server and the request made to it.
$_ENV	Contains all environment variables set by the web server.

The content of the variables $_GET, $_POST, $_COOKIE, $_SERVER, and $_ENV is included in the output generated by the phpinfo function. This function also displays the general settings of the PHP configuration file, php.ini, along with other information regarding PHP.

```
phpinfo(); // display PHP information
```

CHAPTER 24

Cookies

A *cookie* is a small file kept on the client's computer that can be used to store data relating to that user.

Creating Cookies

To create a cookie, the setcookie function is used. This function must be called before any output is sent to the browser. It has three mandatory parameters that contain the name, value, and expiration date of the cookie.

```
setcookie("lastvisit", date("H:i:s"), time() + 60*60);
```

The value here is set with the date function, which returns a string formatted according to the specified format string. The expiration date is measured in seconds and is usually set relative to the current time in seconds retrieved through the time function. In this example, the cookie expires after one hour.

Cookie Array

Once the cookie has been set for a user, this cookie is sent along the next time that user views the page; it can then be accessed through the $_COOKIE array.

```
if (isset($_COOKIE['lastvisit']))
  echo "Last visit: " . $_COOKIE['lastvisit'];
```

Deleting Cookies

A cookie can be deleted manually by re-creating that same cookie with an old expiration date. It is then removed when the browser is closed.

```
setcookie("lastvisit", 0, 0);
```

CHAPTER 25

Sessions

A *session* provides a way to make variables accessible across multiple web pages. Unlike cookies, session data is stored on the server.

Starting a Session

To begin a session, the session_start function is used. This function must appear before any output is sent to the web page.

```php
<?php session_start(); ?>
```

The session_start function sets a cookie on the client's computer, containing an id used to associate the client with the session. If the client already has an ongoing session, the function resumes that session instead of starting a new one.

Session Array

With the session started, the $_SESSION array is used to store session data as well as retrieve it. As an example, the page view count is stored with the following code. The first time the page is viewed, the session element is initialized to one.

```php
if(isset($_SESSION['views']))
  $_SESSION['views'] += 1;
else
  $_SESSION['views'] = 1;
```

This element can now be retrieved from any page on the domain as long as session_start is called on the top of that page.

```php
echo 'Views: ' . $_SESSION['views'];
```

Deleting a Session

A session is guaranteed to last until the user leaves the web site; then, the garbage collector is free to delete that session. To manually remove a session variable, the unset function can be used. For removing all session variables, there is the session_destroy function.

```
unset($_SESSION['views']); // destroy session variable
session_destroy();         // destroy session
```

CHAPTER 26

Namespaces

Namespaces provide a way to avoid naming conflicts and to group namespace members into a hierarchy. Any code may be contained within a namespace, but only four code constructs are affected: classes, interfaces, functions, and constants.

Creating Namespaces

A construct that is not included in a namespace belongs to the global namespace.

```
// Global code/namespace
class MyClass {}
```

To assign the construct to another namespace, a namespace directive is defined. Any code constructs below the namespace directive belong to that namespace. The naming convention for namespaces is all lowercase.

```
namespace my;

// Belongs to my namespace
class MyClass {}
```

A script file containing namespaced code must declare the namespace at the top of the file before any other code, markup, or whitespace. Declare statements are an exception to this because they must be placed before namespace declarations.

```
<?php
namespace my;
class MyClass {}
?>
<html><body></body></html>
```

Nested Namespaces

Namespaces can be nested any number of levels deep to further define the namespace hierarchy. Like directories and files in Windows, namespaces and their members are separated with a backslash character.

```
namespace my\sub;
class MyClass {} // my\sub\MyClass
```

Alternative Syntax

Alternatively, namespaces may be defined with the bracketed syntax commonly used in other programming languages. Just as with the regular syntax, no text or code may exist outside of the namespace.

```
<?php
namespace my
{
  class MyClass {}
?>
<html><body></body></html>
<?php }?>
```

Multiple namespaces can be declared in the same file, although this is not considered good coding practice. If global code is to be combined with namespaced code, then the bracketed syntax must be used. The global code is then enclosed in an unnamed namespace block.

```
// Namespaced code
namespace my
{
  const PI = 3.14;
}

// Global code
namespace
{
  echo my\PI; // "3.14"
}
```

Unlike other PHP constructs, the same namespace may be defined in more than one file. This allows namespace members to be split up across multiple files.

Referencing Namespaces

A namespace member can be referred to in three ways: fully qualified, qualified, and unqualified. The fully qualified name can always be used. It consists of the global prefix operator (\), followed by the namespace path and the member. The global prefix operator indicates that the path is relative to the global namespace.

```
namespace my
{
  class MyClass {}
}

namespace other
{
  // Fully qualified name
  $obj = new \my\MyClass();
}
```

The qualified name includes the namespace path, but not the global prefix operator. Therefore, it can only be used if the wanted member is defined in a namespace below the current namespace in the hierarchy.

```
namespace my
{
  class MyClass {}
}

namespace
{
  // Qualified name
  $obj = new my\MyClass();
}
```

The member name alone, or unqualified name, may only be used within the namespace that defines the member.

```
namespace my
{
  class MyClass {}

  // Unqualified name
  $obj = new MyClass();
}
```

Unqualified class and interface names only resolve to the current namespace. In contrast, if an unqualified function or constant does not exist in the current namespace, they will try to resolve to any global function or constant by the same name.

109

```
namespace
{
  function myPrint() { echo 'global'; }
}

namespace my
{
  // Falls back to global namespace
  myPrint(); // "global"
}
```

Alternatively, the global prefix operator can be used to explicitly refer to the global member. This would be necessary if the current namespace contained a function with the same name.

```
namespace my
{
  function myPrint() { echo 'local'; }

  \myPrint(); // "global"
  myPrint();  // "local"
}
```

Namespace Aliases

Aliases shorten qualified names to improve readability of the source code. The names for classes, interfaces, and namespaces can be shortened. An alias is defined with a use directive, which must be placed after the namespace name in the topmost scope of the file.

```
namespace my;
class MyClass {}

namespace foo;
use my\MyClass as MyAlias;
$obj = new MyAlias();
```

With the bracketed syntax, any use directives are placed after the opening curly bracket in the topmost scope.

```
namespace foo;
{
  use my\MyClass as MyAlias;
  $obj = new MyAlias();
}
```

The as clause may optionally be left out to import the member under its current name.

```
namespace foo;
use \my\MyClass;
$obj = new MyClass();
```

It is not possible to mass-import the members of another namespace. However, there is a syntactical shortcut for importing multiple members in the same use statement.

```
namespace foo;
use my\Class1 as C1, my\Class2 as C2;
```

PHP 7 further simplified this syntax by allowing use declarations to be grouped within curly brackets.

```
namespace foo;
use my\{ Class1 as C1, Class2 as C2 };
```

In addition to classes, interfaces, and namespaces, PHP 5.6 extended the use construct to support function and constant aliases. These are imported with the use function and use const constructs, respectively.

```
namespace my\space {
  const C = 5;
  function f() {}
}

namespace {
  use const my\space\C;
  use function my\space\f;
}
```

Keep in mind that aliases only apply to the script file that defines them. Therefore, an imported file does not inherit the parent file's aliases.

Namespace Keyword

The namespace keyword can be used as a constant that evaluates to the current namespace or an empty string in global code. It may be used to explicitly refer to the current namespace.

```
namespace my\name
{
  function myPrint() { echo 'Hi'; }
}
```

```
namespace my
{
  namespace\name\myPrint(); // "Hi"
  name\myPrint();           // "Hi"
}
```

Namespace Guideline

As the number of components involved in a web application grow, so too increases the potential for name clashes. One solution for this is to prefix names with the name of the component. However, this creates long names, which reduces readability of the source code. For this reason, PHP 5.3 introduced namespaces, which allow developers to group code for each component into separately named containers.

CHAPTER 27

References

A *reference* is an alias that allows two different variables to write to the same value. There are three operations that can be performed with references: assign by reference, pass by reference, and return by reference.

Assign by Reference

A reference is assigned by placing an ampersand (&) before the variable that is to be bound.

```
$x = 5;
$r = &$x; // r is a reference to x
$s =& $x; // alternative syntax
```

The reference then becomes an alias for that variable and can be used exactly as if it was the original variable.

```
$r = 10; // assign value to $r/$x
echo $x; // "10"
```

Pass by Reference

In PHP, function arguments are passed by value by default. This means that a local copy of the variable is passed; so if the copy is changed, it will not affect the original variable.

```
function myFunc($x) { $x .= ' World'; }
```

```
$x = 'Hello';
myFunc($x); // value of x is passed
echo $x;    // "Hello"
```

© Mikael Olsson 2016
M. Olsson, *PHP 7 Quick Scripting Reference*, DOI 10.1007/978-1-4842-1922-5_27

To allow a function to modify an argument, it must be passed by reference. This is done by adding an ampersand before the parameter's name in the function definition.

```
function myFunc(&$x) { $x .= ' World'; }

$x = 'Hello';
myFunc($x); // reference to x is passed
echo $x;    // "Hello World"
```

Object variables are also passed by value by default. However, what is actually passed is a pointer to the object data, not the data itself. Therefore, changes to the object's members affect the original object, but replacing the object variable with the assignment operator only creates a local variable.

```
class MyClass { public $x = 1; }

function modifyVal($o)
{
  $o->x = 5;
  $o = new MyClass(); // new local object
}

$o = new MyClass();
modifyVal($o);        // pointer to object is passed
echo $o->x;           // "5"
```

In contrast, when an object variable is passed by reference, it is not only possible to change its properties, but also to replace the entire object and have the change propagate back to the original object variable.

```
class MyClass { public $x = 1; }

function modifyRef(&$o)
{
  $o->x = 5;
  $o = new MyClass(); // new object
}

$o = new MyClass();
modifyRef($o);        // reference to object is passed
echo $o->x;           // "1"
```

Return by Reference

A variable can be assigned a reference from a function by having that function return by reference. The syntax for returning a reference is to place the ampersand before the function name. In contrast to pass by reference, the ampersand is also used when calling the function to bind the reference.

```
class MyClass
{
  public $val = 10;

  function &getVal()
  {
    return $this->val;
  }
}

$obj = new MyClass();
$myVal = &$obj->getVal();
```

Bear in mind that references should not be used merely for performance reasons, because the PHP engine takes care of such optimizations on its own. Only use references when you have a need for reference-type behavior.

CHAPTER 28

Advanced Variables

In addition to being a container for data, PHP variables have other features that are examined in this chapter. These are features that are not commonly used but are good to know about.

Curly Syntax

A variable name can be explicitly specified by enclosing it in curly brackets. This is known as *curly* or *complex syntax*. To illustrate, the following code outputs the variable even though it appears in the middle of a word.

```
$fruit = 'Apple';
echo "Two {$fruit}s"; // "Two Apples"
```

More importantly, the curly syntax is useful for forming variable names out of expressions. Consider the following code, which uses the curly syntax to construct names for three variables.

```
for ($i = 1; $i <= 3; $i++)
  ${'x'.$i} = $i;

echo "$x1 $x2 $x3"; // "1 2 3"
```

The curly syntax is required here because the expression needs to be evaluated in order to form a valid variable name. If the expression has only a single variable, the curly brackets are not needed.

```
for ($i = 'a'; $i <= 'c'; $i++)
  $$i = $i;

echo "$a $b $c"; // "a b c"
```

This syntax is known as a *variable variable* in PHP.

© Mikael Olsson 2016
M. Olsson, *PHP 7 Quick Scripting Reference*, DOI 10.1007/978-1-4842-1922-5_28

Variable Variable Names

A variable variable is a variable whose name can be changed through code. As an example, consider the following regular variable.

```
$a = 'foo';
```

This variable's value can be used as a variable name by placing an additional dollar sign before it.

```
$$a = 'bar';
```

The value of $a, which is foo, now becomes an alternative name for the $$a variable.

```
echo $foo; // "bar"
echo $$a;  // "bar"
```

An example usage for this would be to generate variables from an array.

```
$arr = array('a' => 'Foo', 'b' => 'Bar');

foreach ($arr as $key => $value)
{
  $$key = $value;
}

echo "$a $b"; // "Foo Bar"
```

Variable Function Names

By placing parentheses after a variable, its value is evaluated as the name for a function.

```
function myPrint($s) { echo $s; }

$func = 'myPrint';
$func('Hello'); // "Hello"
```

This behavior does not work with built-in language constructs, such as echo.

```
echo('Hello');  // "Hello"

$func = 'echo';
$func('Hello'); // error
```

Variable Class Names

Similar to variable function names, classes can be referenced using string variables. This functionality was introduced in PHP 5.3.

```
class MyClass {}

$classname = 'MyClass';
$obj = new $classname();
```

The mechanism of accessing code entities via strings and string variables also works for members of a class or an instance.

```
class MyClass
{
  public $myProperty = 10;
}

$obj = new MyClass();
echo $obj->{'myProperty'}; // "10"
```

CHAPTER 29

Error Handling

An error is a mistake in the code that the developer needs to fix. When an error occurs in PHP, the default behavior is to display the error message in the browser. This message includes the file name, line number, and error description in order to help the developer correct the problem.

While compile and parse errors are typically easy to detect and fix, run-time errors can be harder to find because they may only occur in certain situations and for reasons beyond the developer's control. Consider the following code that attempts to open a file for reading using the fopen function.

```
$handle = fopen('myfile.txt', 'r');
```

It relies on the assumption that the requested file will always be there. If, for any reason, the file is not there or is otherwise inaccessible, the function will generate an error.

```
Warning: fopen(myfile.txt):
failed to open stream: No such file or directory in
C:\xampp\htdocs\mypage.php on line 2
```

Once an error has been detected, it should be corrected, even if it only occurs in exceptional situations.

Correcting Errors

There are two ways to correct this error. The first way is to check to make sure that the file can be read before attempting to open it. PHP conveniently provides the is_readable function for this task, which returns true if the specified file exists and is readable.

```
if (is_readable('myfile.txt'))
  $handle = fopen('myfile.txt', 'r');
```

© Mikael Olsson 2016
M. Olsson, *PHP 7 Quick Scripting Reference*, DOI 10.1007/978-1-4842-1922-5_29

The second way is to use the error control operator (@). When prepended to an expression, this operator suppresses any error messages that might be generated by that expression. Either way works to remove the warning.

```
$handle = @fopen('myfile.txt', 'r');
```

To determine if the file was opened successfully, the return value needs to be examined. Looking at the documentation,[1] you can find that fopen returns false on error.

```
if ($handle === false)
{
  echo 'File not found.';
}
```

If this is not the case, then the content of the file can be read with the fread function. This function reads the number of bytes specified in the second argument from the file handler given in the first argument.

```
else
{
  // Read the content of the whole file
  $content = fread($handle, filesize('myfile.txt'));

  // Close the file handler
  fclose($handle);
}
```

Once the file handler is no longer needed, it is good practice to close it with fclose; although PHP also automatically closes the file after the script has finished.

Error Levels

PHP provides several built-in constants for describing different error levels. Table 29-1 includes some of the more important ones.

---

[1]http://www.php.net/manual/en/function.fopen.php

Table 29-1. *Error Levels*

Name	Description
E_ERROR	Fatal run-time error. Execution is halted.
E_WARNING	Non-fatal run-time error.
E_NOTICE	Run-time notice about possible error.
E_USER_ERROR	Fatal user-generated error.
E_USER_WARNING	Non-fatal user-generated warning.
E_USER_NOTICE	User-generated notice.
E_COMPILE_ERROR	Fatal compile-time error.
E_PARSE	Compile-time parsing error.
E_STRICT	Suggested change to ensure forward compatibility.
E_ALL	All errors, except E_STRICT prior to PHP 5.4.

The first three of these levels represent run-time errors generated by the PHP engine. The following are some examples of operations that trigger these errors.

```
// E_NOTICE - Use of unassigned variable
$a = $x;

// E_WARNING - Missing file
$b = fopen('missing.txt', 'r');

// E_ERROR - Missing function
$c = missing();
```

Error-Handling Environment

PHP provides a few configuration directives for setting up the error-handling environment. The error_reporting function sets which errors PHP reports through the internal error handler. The error level constants have bitmask values. This allows them to be combined and subtracted using bitwise operators, as shown here.

```
error_reporting(E_ALL | ~E_NOTICE); // all but E_NOTICE
```

The error reporting level can also be changed permanently in php.ini. The default value found in php.ini varies between servers, but for an XAMPP server, it is set to display all error messages. This is a good setting to have during development and it can be set programmatically by placing the following line of code at the start of the script. Note that E_STRICT is added, because this error level was not included in E_ALL until PHP 5.4.

```
// During development
error_reporting(E_ALL | E_STRICT);
```

When the web app goes live, raw error messages should be hidden away from users. This is done with the display_errors directive. It determines whether errors are printed to the web page by the internal error handler. The default value is to print them, but when the web site is live, it is a good idea to hide any potential raw error messages.

```
// During production
ini_set('display_errors','0');
```

Another directive related to the error-handling environment is the log_errors directive. It sets whether error messages are recorded in the server's error log. This directive is disabled by default, but it is a good idea to enable it during development to keep track of errors.

```
// During development
ini_set('log_errors','1');
```

The ini_set function sets the value of a configuration option. Alternatively, these options can all be permanently set in the php.ini configuration file instead of in the script files.

Custom Error Handlers

The internal error handler can be overridden with a custom error handler. This is the preferred method for handling errors because it allows you to abstract the raw errors with friendly, custom error messages to the end users.

A custom error handler is defined using the set_error_handler function. This function accepts two arguments: a callback function that is called when the error is raised, and optionally, the error levels that the function handles.

```
set_error_handler('myError', E_ALL | E_STRICT);
```

If no error levels are specified, the error handler is set to handle all errors, including E_STRICT. However, a user-defined error handler is only actually able to handle run-time errors, and only run-time errors other than E_ERROR. Keep in mind that changes to the error_reporting setting do not affect the custom error handler, only the internal one.

The callback function requires two parameters: the error level and error description. Optional parameters include the file name, line number, and error context, which is an array containing every variable in the scope that the error was triggered in.

```php
function myError($errlvl, $errdesc, $errfile, $errline)
{
  switch($errlvl)
  {
    case E_USER_ERROR:
      error_log("Error: $errdesc", 1, 'me@example.com');
      require_once('my_error_page.php');
      return true;
  }
  return false;
}
```

This example function handles errors of level E_USER_ERROR. When such an error occurs, an email is sent to the specified address and a custom error page is displayed. By returning false from the function for other errors, they are handled by the internal error handler instead.

Raising Errors

PHP provides the trigger_error function for raising errors. It has one required argument, the error message, and a second optional argument specifying the error level. The error level must be one of the three E_USER levels, with E_USER_NOTICE being the default level.

```php
if( !isset($myVar) )
  trigger_error('$myVar not set'); // E_USER_NOTICE
```

Triggering errors is useful when you have a custom error handler in place, allowing you to combine the handling of both custom errors and errors raised by PHP.

CHAPTER 30

Exception Handling

PHP 5 introduced *exceptions*, a built-in mechanism for handling program failures within the context in which they occur. Unlike errors, which generally need to be fixed by the developer, exceptions are handled by the script. They represent an irregular run-time situation that should have been expected as a possibility and which the script should be able to handle on its own.

Try-catch Statement

To handle an exception, it must be caught using a try-catch statement. This statement consists of a try block containing the code that may cause the exception, and one or more catch clauses.

```
try
{
  $div = invert(0);
}
catch (LogicException $e) {}
```

If the try block successfully executes, the program then continues running after the try-catch statement. However, if an exception occurs, the execution is then passed to the first catch block able to handle that exception type.

Throwing Exceptions

When a situation occurs that a function cannot recover from, it can generate an exception to signal to the caller that the function has failed. This is done using the throw keyword, followed by a new instance of the Exception class or a child class of Exception, such as LogicException.[1]

---

[1] http://www.php.net/manual/en/spl.exceptions.php

© Mikael Olsson 2016
M. Olsson, *PHP 7 Quick Scripting Reference*, DOI 10.1007/978-1-4842-1922-5_30

```
function invert($x)
{
  if ($x == 0)
    throw new LogicException('Division by zero');

  return 1 / $x;
}
```

Catch Block

In the previous example, the catch block is set to handle the built-in LogicException type. If the code in the try block could throw more kinds of exceptions, multiple catch blocks can be used, allowing different exceptions to be handled in different ways.

```
catch (LogicException $e) {}
catch (RuntimeException $e) {}
// ...
```

To catch a more specific exception, the catch block needs to be placed before exceptions that are more general. For example, the LogicException inherits from Exception, so the LogicException needs to be caught first.

```
catch (LogicException $e) {}
catch (Exception $e) {}
```

The catch clause defines an exception object. This object can be used to obtain more information about the exception, such as a description of the exception using the getMessage method.

```
catch (LogicException $e)
{
  echo $e->getMessage(); // "Division by zero"
}
```

Finally Block

PHP 5.5 introduced the finally block, which can be added as the last clause in a try-catch statement. This block is used to clean up resources allocated in the try block. It always executes whether or not there is an exception.

```
$resource = myopen();
try { myuse($resource); }
catch(Exception $e) {}
finally { myfree($resource); }
```

Rethrowing Exceptions

Sometimes an exception cannot be handled where it is first caught. It can then be rethrown using the throw keyword followed by the exception object.

```
try { $div = invert(0); }
catch (LogicException $e) { throw $e; }
```

The exception then propagates up the caller stack until it is caught by another try-catch statement. If the exception is never caught, it becomes an error of level E_ERROR, which halts the script, unless an uncaught exception handler has been defined.

Uncaught Exception Handler

The set_exception_handler function allows any uncaught exceptions to be caught. It takes a single argument, which is the callback function that is raised for such an event.

```
set_exception_handler('myException');
```

The callback function only needs one parameter, the exception object that was thrown.

```
function myException($e)
{
  $file = 'exceptionlog.txt';
  file_put_contents($file,$e->getMessage(),FILE_APPEND);
  require_once('my_error_page.php');
  exit;
}
```

Because this exception handler is called outside the context where the exception occurred, recovering from the exception would be difficult. Instead, this example handler writes the exception to a log file and displays an error page. To stop further execution of the script, the built-in exit construct is used. It is synonymous with the die construct and optionally takes a string argument that is printed before the script is halted.

Errors and Exceptions

Whereas exceptions are thrown with the intention of being handled by the script, errors are generated to inform the developer that there is a mistake in the code. When it comes to problems that occur at run-time, the exception mechanism is generally considered superior. However, since it was not introduced until PHP 5, all internal functions still use the error mechanism. For user-defined functions, the developer is free to choose either mechanism. Keep in mind that errors cannot be caught by try-catch statements. Likewise, exceptions do not trigger error handlers.

CHAPTER 31

Assertions

Assert is a debugging feature that can be used during development to ensure that a condition is always true. Any expression can be asserted, as long as it evaluates to either true or false.

```php
// Make sure $myVar is set
assert(isset($myVar));
```

Code assertions like this help validate that there are no execution paths that break the specified assumption. If this occurs, a warning showing the file and line number of the assertion is displayed, which makes it easy to locate and fix the mistake in the code.

```
Warning: assert(): Assertion failed in C:\xampp\htdocs\mypage.php on line 3
```

A description of the assertion may be included, which is displayed if the assertion fails. Support for this second parameter was added in PHP 5.4.8.

```php
assert(isset($myVar), '$myVar not set');
```

As of PHP 7, the second parameter can also be an exception object to be thrown if the assertion fails. By default, an AssertionError is thrown when an assertion fails.

```php
assert(false, new AssertionError('Assert failed'));
```

Assert Performance

Assertions can be turned off using the assert_options function by setting the ASSERT_ACTIVE option to zero. This means that assertions do not need to be removed from the code after debugging is finished and the development code becomes production code.

```php
// Disable assertions
assert_options(ASSERT_ACTIVE, 0);
```

© Mikael Olsson 2016
M. Olsson, *PHP 7 Quick Scripting Reference*, DOI 10.1007/978-1-4842-1922-5_31

A condition passed to an assertion is always evaluated, even if assertions are turned off. To avoid this extra overhead in production code, the condition can be passed as a string instead, which is then evaluated by assert.

```
assert('isset($myVar)');
```

Passing the condition as a string has the added benefit of including the string in the warning shown when the assertion fails.

```
Warning: assert(): Assertion "isset($myVar)" failed in C:\xampp\htdocs\
mypage.php on line 3
```

In PHP 7, assert became a language construct, as opposed to a function, allowing for zero performance loss from including assertions in production code. The way to skip assertions completely in PHP 7 is to set the zend.assertions configuration directive to -1 in the php.ini configuration file.

Index

© Mikael Olsson 2016
M. Olsson, *PHP 7 Quick Scripting Reference*, DOI 10.1007/978-1-4842-1922-5

Get the eBook for only $5!

Why limit yourself?

Now you can take the weightless companion with you wherever you go and access your content on your PC, phone, tablet, or reader.

Since you've purchased this print book, we're happy to offer you the eBook in all 3 formats for just $5.

Convenient and fully searchable, the PDF version enables you to easily find and copy code—or perform examples by quickly toggling between instructions and applications. The MOBI format is ideal for your Kindle, while the ePUB can be utilized on a variety of mobile devices.

To learn more, go to www.apress.com/companion or contact support@apress.com.

Printed by Books on Demand, Germany